Desperate for Authenticity

A Critical Analysis of the Feminist Theology of Virginia Ramey Mollenkott

Patricia Hawley

Foreword by Virginia Ramey Mollenkott

UNIVERSITY PRESS OF AMERICA, ® INC.
Lanham • Boulder • New York • Toronto • Plymouth, UK

Library of Congress Control Number: 2010927417
ISBN: 978-0-7618-5181-3 (paperback : alk. paper)
eISBN: 978-0-7618-5181-3

Contents

Foreword

About a year ago, I received by email the final chapter of a forthcoming book critiquing my theology and its close relationship to my life-journey. (Everyone's outlook is always strongly affected by the circumstances they have experienced, but people who are comfortable within a large, respected, normative communities often imagine that their point of view is objective and is the ultimate truth for everyone. Hence they tend to be unaware of the fact that their circumstances have dictated their perspectives just as much as my circumstances have dictated mine.)

I read the critique, written by Dr. Patricia Hawley, a professor at the New Orleans (Southern) Baptist Theological Seminary, and then wrote to her about the ways in which I felt she had misrepresented my point of view. She wrote back graciously, expressing her sincere desire to dialogue with me so that when we differed, it would be about genuine difference, respectfully expressed, and not a series of attacks and counterattacks concerning things we did not actually write, say, or believe.

Subsequently, Dr. Hawley sent me her entire book, which I read, annotated with my differing perspectives, and returned to her by mail. We had planned for her to visit me in my New Jersey Retirement Community so we could talk face to face, but unexpected circumstances (including the death of Trish's mother) made the visit impossible. Anyone seeking full disclosure of my worldview would of course have to read my original books and articles, but essentially Dr. Hawley has provided a good illustration of how to represent someone's radically different perspectives without contemptuous or disrespectful judgmentalism. Both Dr. Hawley and I are hoping that when taken as a whole, this foreword and the book that follows will demonstrate the largely forgotten art of mutually respectful dialogue.

To begin, I must take issue with the statement (derived from Pamela Cochran) that the Evangelical and Ecumenical Women's Caucus "drifted into inclusivist goddess worship" (p.6). As a founding and still active member of that organization, I can testify that we often make use of biblical images of God as female (for instance, as the Mother of those who are "born again," according to John 3:3-6: we are "born of" our mothers). But we have never worshipped a goddess. As monotheists, we have worshipped the One God who is "above all, through all, and in you all." (Eph. 4:6, KJV) When we use feminine pronouns to match the female images of God in the biblical precedent, we no more mean that God is literally female than more traditional evangelicals mean God is literally male when they speak of "God Himself," as Dr. Hawley occasionally does (p.148). Presumably, we all agree that God is Spirit, as we are told in John 4:24.

Secondly, I have often pointed out that it is a mistake to emphasize God's immanence ("through all" and "in all") to the exclusion of God's transcendence ("above all"). So when Dr. Hawley says that I teach that "God is everything and in everything" (p.180) without providing my balancing emphasis on God's transcendence, she is turning me into a pantheist rather than a panentheist. To me, there's a very important distinction between the two.

Thirdly, on p. 14 Dr. Hawley writes that "historically, Christians believed that [Genesis 19, the story of Sodom] condemned the sin of homosexuality." Unfortunately, like many evangelicals, she discounts the historical records uncovered by scholars like Mark Jordan (Harvard), John Boswell (Yale), Dale Martin (Yale), and Theodore Jennings, Jr. (Chicago Theological Seminary). The Bible itself identifies the sin of Sodom as unjust oppression and inhospitality (Isaiah 1:9 and 17; Matt. 10:11-15; Luke 10:8-12; Romans 9:29). I often wonder why evangelicals who clams the Bible as their ultimate authority would insist that the sin of Sodom was homosexuality, when the Bible consistently makes an entirely different claim, one that seems to condemn the greedy excesses of capitalism.

It was not until the 6th century after Christ and 500 years after Paul wrote his epistles that Christianity began to adopt into its own discourses some of the homophobia of Plato's pre-Christian Laws. And it was not until the 12th century than the Christian hierarchy began to insist on rejection of same sex love as an essential aspect of Christian doctrine. So in our book *is the Homosexual My Neighbor?* Letha Dawson Scanzoni and I aw ourselves as returning to early Christians interpretations of Sodom, rather than developing something new and contrary to Christian tradition. And despite Dr. Hawley's statement on p. 125, I have never "affirmed" the "fallen nature" or "redefined the biblical position" so that all homosexual practices are acceptable (p.195).

I have defended love that is responsible, respectful, and mutually supportive, whether it be same-sex or other-sex intimacy.

Finally, and most importantly: as a person who spent 44 years teaching literary interpretation in college and graduate school, I must object to Dr. Hawley's emphasis that I moved away from Scripture as "the authoritative guide for living" and turned instead to "reason and experience as determinative" (p. 15 and elsewhere). Nobody can read any text without making use of reason to interpret its meaning; and nobody can approach any text devoid of the context of their life experience and preconceptions learned from their teachers and comrades life journey. If we spend our entire life in a community that interprets Scripture as we ourselves do, and if we are able to fit our behaviors comfortably within that community, we tend to develop the illusion that our view of Scripture is THE view of Scripture, the only set of interpretations worth bothering with. The illusion is possible because everybody in our interpretive community joins us in ignoring the Bible passages that might make us uncomfortable by casting doubt upon our community's tacitly accepted point of view. But I was called and gifted to study theology in a community that denied women any voice in theology. I was born lesbian in a community that saw homosexuals as deliberately defiant toward God. I was born with many "masculine" leadership traits in a community that required women to be subservient to men and to obey the gender roles and rules of "total femininity" I could have walked away from Christianity, but instead I used the abilities I had been given to work and study my way into what seems to me to be an open, clear, responsible way of life as a follower of Jesus the Christ, whom I dearly love.

So when Mary Kassian says I have made "the feminist mistake" of approaching the Bible with a lens of liberation (cited here on p. 182), she is the voice of a normative community's shared privilege. Kassian seems unaware that she too approaches the Bible from her own context, perhaps because she is relatively comfortable within her interpretive community's rules and roles. My experience is more like that of Dr. Katherine Bushnell, who felt called to be a medical missionary but resented her community's teaching that women must always be secondary to men. She deliberately removed the blinders her community assumed everyone should wear and focused on the Scriptures that might dislocate or demolish what she had been taught. The result was Dr. Bushnell's find book *God's Word to Women* (1900-) and her service as a medical missionary to China.

All this is by way of responding to Dr. Hawley's question of why I "allowed" so many outside authoritative influences on my hermeneutics" (p. 196 and elsewhere). From my perspective, I have answered that question in everyone of my books and articles, by defining my social location as carefully and honestly as possible in order to take full responsibility for the conclusions at which I have arrived (i.e., giving a "reason of the hope that is in [me], I Peter 3:15). I challenge people like Pamela Cochran, Mary Kassian, John Piper, Rick Warren, Raymond Ortland, George Alan Rekers, and Wayne Grudem to do the same.

To summarize: the crux of my differences with Dr. Hawley is highlighted by her questioning how I could "uphold biblical authority" without "adhering to the basic principles and practices of an evangelical Christian" (p.187) and her confidence that "If a belief system does not profess that the only way to salvation is through Jesus Christ, it is not cohesive with orthodox Christianity" (p.190). Perhaps Dr. Hawley has overlooked the many deeply spiritual Christians through the ages who have interpreted the Bible in ways that differ from those of contemporary right-wing evangelicalism. For instance, her statement that Jesus died on the cross because "it was the only way to satisfy the wrath of God" (p.194) would probably have satisfied Anselm's 11th century theory of *Why God Became Man*, but it would have surprised many earlier Christians as well as many more recent ones.

Dr. Hawley and I differ radically on our interpretation of what would be a healing response to homosexuality (p.197). Like anyone who has found a relatively comfortable niche in a normative group, she assumes a "Good Samaritan" would try to heal the mane who'd been attacked by thieves by taking steps to make him like herself and the others in her interpretive community. But I, like anyone from a despised and outcast category, perceive healing to be an active, supportive affirmation of the person I was created to be before the thieves attacked and wounded me and left me to die in a ditch. For people in minority groups, the Big Questions always have to be, "Who profits from my interpretation?" and "Who gets to define what a loving response looks like?"

There are other differences I could discuss, but this is Dr. Hawley's book, not mine. So I will go silent now and invite readers to read on and think these matters through for themselves.

Virginia Ramey Mollenkott, Ph.D.
Professor of English Emeritus
The William Paterson University of New Jersey
December 28, 2009

Chapter One

Research Concerns

"We acknowledge that we have encouraged men to prideful dominations and women to irresponsible passivity. So we call both men and women to mutual submission and active discipleship."[1] At the conclusion of the first informal gathering of the Evangelicals for Social Action, Nancy Hardesty, an early religious feminist leader, drafted this statement on the group's concern for the equal treatment of women. The events that followed that day in 1973 contributed to the beginning of a shift in evangelicalism.[2] New thought on the doctrines of manhood and womanhood contributed to this shift in evangelicalism; this book chronicles some of those changes and argues for the importance of a critical analysis of the theology of Virginia Ramey Mollenkott, a pioneer leader in the religious feminist movement.

INTRODUCTION TO THE RESEARCH PROBLEM

The cultural crises in the United States during the 1960s and 1970s took its toll on young evangelical leaders. Evangelicalism was at a turning point in its history. Social concerns rampant in secular culture had not left the church untouched. One of the leaders in the new era of evangelicalism, Virginia Ramey Mollenkott, led women and men to embracing this new position later identified as "religious feminism." To understand her influence and importance, it is helpful to understand the development of the movement itself.

A Brief History of Feminism in the Religious Setting

By the early 1970s, many younger evangelicals felt the need to gather to discuss a Christian response to the questions raised in the civil rights movement.

Attendees of this group were well educated Christians who felt a responsibility to address the cultural issues of their day.[3] This meeting came to be known as the Evangelicals for Social Action.[4] While Mollenkott was not present at this initial meeting, her contributions were influenced by its organization.

Evangelicals for Social Action

Only six women were invited to this meeting, and most of them were the wives of attendees; however, the question of the role of women arose as it pertained to the social concerns of the meeting.[5] The statement written by Nancy Hardesty and appearing at the beginning of this chapter served as a first attempt to address sexism in the evangelical church.[6] The following year the events of the Evangelicals for Social Action led to the formation of the Evangelical Women's Caucus (EWC). This group was made up of women and a few men who were solely concerned with the treatment of women in society and particularly in the church.[7]

Evangelical Women's Caucus

A task force of women from the Evangelicals for Social Action was formed to address the issues raised at the 1973 meeting. These women formed a steering committee out of which came organizational bylaws and structure.[8] The first Evangelical Women's Caucus met Thanksgiving weekend of 1975.[9] The theme of their conference was "Women in Transition: A Biblical Approach to Feminism," with keynote speaker Virginia Ramey Mollenkott addressing "the need to recognize that the patriarchal culture of biblical times was not authoritative for the present day."[10] With the conviction that patriarchy was oppressive for women and unbiblical, the religious feminist movement began.

From 1975 to 1983 the Evangelical Women's Caucus (EWC) grew financially and numerically.[11] Women and men from all over the United States joined the movement to link secular feminist ideology with a biblical response. In their official statement of faith, adopted in 1978, the Evangelical Women's Caucus stated its purpose at that time was to "call both women and men to mutual submission and active discipleship."[12] The idea of mutual submission was a new term being developed among the biblical feminists; however, for those people who ascribed to the views of the EWC, this term became synonymous with what they called the equal treatment of the sexes.[13] It served as a rallying point for the first years of the Evangelical Women's Caucus.

The next three national EWC conferences contributed to the development of the organization. In 1979, the conference theme was "Called by Christ for the Sake of the Church and the World" and the meeting was held in Grand Rapids, Michigan. "Women and the Ministry of Reconciliation" was the theme in 1980 at the meeting in Sarasota Springs, New York; and "Women and the Promise of Restoration" was the theme for the 1982 Seattle, Washington conference.[14] Each of these meetings built collectively on the preceding themes. They also served as a time for new people to be introduced to the ideas of the feminist theology and for circulation of new materials that argued their positions.[15] The official newsletter of the EWC was *Daughters of Sarah*.[16]

The progressive ideas of the Evangelical Women's Caucus soon led to points of diversion, however. Among these points was the question of the official position of the caucus on the treatment of homosexuals in the church.[17] In 1978 Virginia Mollenkott and Letha Scanzoni published *Is the Homosexual My Neighbor?* In this book, the authors presented their views on the issue.[18] From the beginning, Mollenkott was at the heart of controversy in the religious feminist movement, and her ideas, along with those of Letha Scanzoni, began an underlying tension in the caucus surrounding the issue of homosexuality which would not be addressed forthrightly for several years.[19] Mollenkott and Scanzoni articulated their argument in terms of moral maturity through loving your neighbor.[20] They argued that to be a relevant church in the twentieth century was to accept and condone homosexuality by granting full civil rights to homosexuals.[21]

Homosexuality, for the members of the EWC, became a "watershed issue" in the years leading up to an organizational split in 1984.[22] The desire of most religious feminist leaders was to avoid addressing this issue for fear of its dividing the movement. In fact, at the 1978 conference there was to be a debate between Scanzoni and Mollenkott (for acceptance of homosexuality) and Don Williams (questioning the full support of homosexuals), but the debate was cancelled for "fear of detracting from the spirit of unity" in the EWC.[23] For several years, then, this question was squelched until the Fresno, California conference in 1986.[24]

Controversy encroached on this conference even before its convening. The previous decision for the ban on resolutions at business meetings of the EWC was literally ignored by Nancy Hardesty, the chair for the business meetings in 1986.[25] On July 8, Hardesty recognized Michelle Borba who introduced a resolution on racial injustice.[26] The third motion of the day was by Anne Eggbroten calling for civil rights for homosexuals:

> I move that, whereas homosexual people are children of God, and because of the biblical mandate of Jesus Christ that we are all created equal in God's sight, and in recognition of the presence of the lesbian minority in Evangelical Women's Caucus International take a firm stand in favor of civil rights protection for homosexual persons.[27]

Several issues made the passing of this resolution controversial; however, the vote was taken and for the first time the Evangelical Women's Caucus was publicly divided over the issue of homosexuality.

The following months unfolded many changes in the Evangelical Women's Caucus. At the concluding plenary address of the Fresno conference Virginia Ramey Mollenkott called for an overall rejection of "heterosexism" in the EWC.[28] Her message to reject outright traditional Christian teachings on sexuality caused more conservative religious feminists of that time, such as Catherine Kroeger and Alvera Mickelson, much concern. In the winter of 1987, the Minnesota regional chapter of the EWC formally broke away from the caucus to form their own organization.[29]

Over time the Evangelical Women's Caucus changed their name to the Evangelical and Ecumenical Women's Caucus, distancing themselves from their evangelical roots.[30] In a survey, as members were asked about the views of the EEWC, two members stated that they did not see it as a "religious organization at all;" while others stated that they thought it was basically no different than its "secular feminist counterparts."[31] The EEWC still exists today, known more widely as Christian Feminism Today.[32]

Christians for Biblical Equality

Based on the structure of John Stott's organization, "Men, Women, and God, International," located at the London Institute for Contemporary Christianity, members who left the EWC soon began to reorganize themselves.[33] By March 1987, the group had planned a two-day conference in St. Paul, Minnesota to discuss their possibilities. By August 1987, the group met in Massachusetts at the home of Richard and Catherine Kroeger to develop their mission statement, faith statement, and constitution.[34]

In July 1989, the group issued a formal position paper called "Men, Women, and Equality."[35] Stated therein was their affirmation that the view of the Bible was the inspired Word of God and of the equality of the sexes. In 1990, the paper was published in the popular periodicals *Christianity Today* and *Leadership*.[36] The leaders of the group were well on their way to forming a more conservative, Christian feminist organization.[37]

In similar fashion to the EWC, the new group, later to be known as Christians for Biblical Equality (CBE), initiated an organizational newsletter called the "Priscilla Papers."[38] This periodical would serve as a scholarly tool to communicate nationally the events and concerns of the group.[39] Centrally focused on the belief in the biblical equality of men and women, the new group of evangelical feminists distanced themselves from the issue of homosexuality.

The first edition, in the fall of 1987, included an article entitled "Who will be real? When will we be free?" by Kari Malcolm which called for men and women in their organization to be "real or set free (which) means looking beyond ourselves and our homes, first to the conservative women in our churches who are not 'real'—not taken seriously."[40] The author also wrote that "our task is to provide friendship, forums for discussion on women's status, information and Bible study on women, written from a conservative perspective about the freedom Christ has given us in the Gospel."[41] The founders of the group carefully communicated that they saw themselves as more "conservative" or not willing to support the civil rights of homosexuals in the church at that time.

The members of CBE held closely to their beliefs in religious feminism; while being simultaneously unwilling to follow the course of their more "progressive" counterparts in the EWC. Chronicling the development of evangelical feminism, historian Pamela Cochran noted several differences in the two groups of feminists. First, the groups from the beginning viewed biblical authority differently; second, they also varied on their hermeneutical principles; and finally they clearly disagreed on their stands on homosexuality with Mollenkott as a clear leader in this difference.[42]

The three issues at the heart of the debate of how to connect feminist ideology with Christianity were biblical authority, hermeneutical principles, and homosexuality. The degree to which one of these issues was emphasized over the other determined the kind of feminist theology to be espoused. Attention now turns to a consideration of these topics and will conclude with the contributions of Virginia Ramey Mollenkott to the historical development and ideological construction of religious feminism.

THREE CENTRAL ISSUES IN FEMINISM
IN THE WORLD OF RELIGION

The development of religious feminism did not occur in a vacuum. Evangelicalism in the decade between 1960 and 1970 experienced growing pains as it faced many of the cultural issues of that day.[43] While concerns outside the church were many and varied, three points of contention within evangelicalism influenced the development of religious feminism. Biblical authority, hermeneutical principles, and the treatment of homosexuals became watershed issues defining historical markers in the religious feminist position. Thoughtful contemplation of each of these issues with a view to the contributions of Virginia Ramey Mollenkott is offered next in this introduction.

The Authority of the Bible

From the beginning, biblical authority played a role in the development of feminist theology.[44] The early religious feminists believed that the Bible was God's Word, and in fact attributed their feminism to its teaching on biblical equality. Letha Scanzoni, an early leader in the movement, wrote, "We did not become feminists and then try to fit our Christianity into feminist ideology. We became feminists because we were Christians."[45] Virginia Mollenkott also attributed her developing belief in feminism to her growth in her Christian theology.[46] For these scholars, the desire to promote equal treatment of women quickly led to alterations in the traditional view of biblical authority.

By the early 1970s, the question of the reliability and inerrancy of Scripture was being debated in the evangelical community.[47] Wanting to address the social concerns of their day, evangelical leaders sought to answer cultural problems with an intelligent faith. The younger evangelicals' social concerns led to integration of academic disciplines outside the traditional theological academy.[48] With this move outside the major disciplines of concern for evangelicalism, the extent of belief for biblical authority became an issue for the younger evangelicals.

"We believe in the Bible's authority and begin with what Scripture has to say about us and about God."[49] In its origins, religious feminism was distinct from secular feminism because of the belief in the authority of Scripture. Unlike their secular counterparts, many early Christian feminists felt "called of the Lord" into feminism to herald equal treatment of women. While early religious feminists began with Scripture, their interpretations of traditional teachings on the roles of men and women illustrated a different understanding of biblical authority.

In *Women, Men, & the Bible*, the first major contribution of Virginia Ramey Mollenkott, she wrote: "Biblical feminism must root itself firmly in the major Bible doctrines of the Trinity, of creation in the image of God, of the incarnation, and of regeneration."[50] Once the decision was made to unite feminist ideology with the teachings of Christianity, religious feminists sought to re-interpret traditional understandings of the roles of men and women. In these words from Mollenkott, she urged her readers to consider these major doctrines in the development of Christian feminism. It is precisely here that the question of biblical authority begins and later turns to the question of hermeneutical principles.

According to Paul K. Jewett, a personal friend and mentor to Mollenkott, in his work, *Man as Male and Female*, the Apostle Paul simply misinterpreted the Genesis teachings when he wrote on women's subordination in the New Testament.[51] Mollenkott agreed with this interpretation and in fact advocated reevaluating all of Scripture through the lens of culture. She argued that the male need for patriarchal rule dictated societal structure and rule; therefore, to regain equal treatment of women and men, culture must "de-absolutize" patriarchy.[52] She implied that the domination of men in leadership roles and the deference of women to men in everyday life must be rejected as the cultural norm. Both Mollenkott and Jewett illustrated the move from a traditional understanding of biblical authority to a newer definition of it. Eventually, the question of biblical authority moved to debate over the use of hermeneutical principles.

The Development of Hermeneutics

While religious feminism was emerging in the 1960s, newer methods of biblical interpretation, or hermeneutics, were also gaining acceptance in the theological academy.[53] This new methodology in biblical interpretation, or higher criticism, called for the consideration of literary structure, date and authorship of biblical texts.[54] As the younger evangelicals sought to meet their social concerns for women, these newer hermeneutical practices aided their attempt to unite Scripture as God's Word, while reinterpreting its teachings on men and women.

Traditional evangelical hermeneutics called for the reading and acceptance of the whole counsel of God as revealed in Scripture.[55] Women's liberation was the central concern for biblical feminists; therefore, this concern controlled the reading and interpretation of instruction on men and women.[56] This change in hermeneutical emphasis led to the revision of many of the key biblical texts to meet the emerging cultural pressures of feminism.[57]

In *Women, Men, & the Bible*, Mollenkott argued that a major concern of Jesus, Peter, and Paul was social justice. She asserted that the message of Scripture should be viewed through these lenses. In other words, because Paul narrowly addressed the cultural situations of his day his teachings were not cross-culturally applicable.[58] Mollenkott wrote:

> Because patriarchy is the cultural background of the scriptures, it is absolutely basic to any feminist reading of the Bible that one cannot absolutize the culture in which the Bible was written. To absolutize something means to regard it as the fundamental or ultimate reality. So to absolutize the biblical culture would mean to assume that the standards of ancient Israel or first-century society represent God's ultimate will for the human race. Instead of making such an assumption, we must make careful distinctions between what is "for our age" and what is "for all time."[59]

If a passage was culturally bound, then its authority was limited only to a particular time and place. As illustrated in this belief, the whole of Scripture was not binding for the faith and practice of Christian feminists.

These men and women also believed that interpretation of revelation was progressive.[60] Since culture was continually changing, the understanding and interpretation of passages dealing with culture did as well. For the religious feminists, these newly accepted hermeneutical practices opened the way for non-traditional interpretations of the Genesis creation story, the teachings of the Apostle Paul, and other major passages that spoke to the roles of men and women. These hermeneutical practices allowed for the development of their positions.

Diversity in the opinions of biblical feminists regarding the authoritative place of Scripture and its interpretation existed from the early development of this position. With the move from the Bible as the authoritative source for instruction and practice of the Christian faith, methodology in biblical interpretation became the defining mark of the biblical feminist position.[61] A leader's perspective about a certain passage and the methodology employed to reach that position dictated the kind of Christian feminist she would be.

Popular culture also dictated the issues to which religious feminists subscribed in their scholarship.[62] It was because of this emphasis that the issue of homosexuality arose. When Mollenkott and Scanzoni published *Is the Homosexual My Neighbor?* in 1978, the question was officially introduced for public debate. Diverse opinions existed, depending on the methodology of biblical interpretation employed by each scholar. For the purposes of this book, the role that the issue of homosexuality played in the development in the religious feminist position is considered next.

The Issue of Homosexuality

"Today the church remains one of the institutions most oppressive to gay people, sometimes opposing even their basic civil rights to jobs, housing, and legal protection."[63] With the publication of *All We're Meant To Be*, by Letha Scanzoni and Nancy Hardesty, several new ideas were introduced into evangelicalism. The debate continued with the publication of *Is the Homosexual My Neighbor?* by Mollenkott and Scanzoni. For the first time, the religious feminist position was put forth in a way that gained a hearing among traditional evangelical leaders. Debate as to its legitimacy continues to this day. However, with its entrance came the debate over the position of the church on the acceptance of homosexuality.

The issue gained little attention until the publication of *Is the Homosexual My Neighbor* by Letha Scanzoni and Virginia Mollenkott in 1978. Not all religious feminists wanted to address this issue publicly; however, its presence within feminist ideology would not allow its avoidance. From the very beginning of the second wave of feminism, sexual identity was at the heart of feminist philosophy; so if the church would unite feminism with Christianity, it would also have to consider its treatment of homosexuals.[64]

While Scanzoni and Mollenkott introduced the topic for discussion in their book, they also presented their position in non-traditional ways. A large portion of their book was an exegetical analysis of the major biblical passages dealing with understanding homosexuality. They reinterpreted many passages traditionally thought to be teachings against homosexuality. An example of this would be their treatment of Genesis 19. They wrote:

> All of this is by way of saying that rather than concentrating on homosexuality, the Sodom story seems to be focusing on two specific evils: (1) violent gang rape, and (2) inhospitality to strangers. . . . Violence—forcing sexual activity

upon another—is the real point of this story. To put it another way: even if the angels had taken on the form of women for their earthly visitation, the desire of the men of Sodom to rape them would have been every bit as evil in the sight of God. And the rain of fire and brimstone would have been every bit as sure.[65]

Historically, Christians believed that this passage condemned the sin of homosexuality. Scanzoni and Mollenkott reinterpreted this passage, however, using newer hermeneutical practices to state that the real sin of the men in Genesis 19 was a lack of hospitality.[66]

On the basis of improper hermeneutical usages, another religious feminist disagreed publicly with Scanzoni and Mollenkott. Don Williams, author of *The Bond that Breaks: Will Homosexuality Split the Church?*, critiqued the exegetical methods used by the two authors to condone homosexuality.[67] He also engaged them at the second Evangelical Women's Caucus by presenting his ideas in a workshop.[68] The authors' emphasis on scientific evidence and reason to support their positions on homosexuality rendered them dangerous in the eyes of more traditional religious feminists, and it eventually led to a schism in the movement to unite feminism with Christianity.[69]

Why was the question of the treatment of homosexuals so vital in the development of the feminist theology? Cultural pressure made the early religious feminists concerned with the topic because of its relevance to issues of the day. Theologically, however, the question of manhood and womanhood is a question related to the image of God first communicated in the book of Genesis. Therefore, any attempt to define them apart would lead to greater questions of truth. The basic tenet of feminism to reject patriarchy was connected to core beliefs about reality, history, and anthropology. When feminist thinkers rejected the historical roles of wife and mother by redefining their identity according to the experience of women rather than the perspective of men, questions of homosexuality was close behind.[70]

Acceptance and affirmation of homosexual orientation was rooted in emphasizing the validity of reason and personal experience rather than Scripture as an authoritative guide to life.[71] Mollenkott argued clearly according to this methodology in many of her books; however in her book called *Transgender Journeys* she and co-author Vanessa Sheridan urged their readers to embrace their sexual orientation and to come out as an act of faith.[72] The religious feminists who argued for the acceptance of this lifestyle did so primarily from newer interpretations of Scripture, which depended on information from scientific evidence rather than from the biblical text.[73] Later evangelical feminists who disagreed with the acceptance of homosexuality did so based on their understanding of hermeneutical principles and biblical inerrancy.

In every way, homosexuality proved to be a watershed issue in the development of religious feminism. It triggered the movement from Scripture as the authoritative guide for living to reason and experience as determinative.

In the interpretation of biblical texts that directly dealt with the issue of homosexuality, it ushered in the usage of newer hermeneutical practices to accept the homosexual lifestyle. One historian of evangelical feminism wrote, "In short, the decisive role of homosexuality in biblical feminism can be traced back to conflicting views of the authority of Scripture."[74]

Within the development of the religious feminist movement, these three issues (biblical authority, hermeneutical practices, and homosexuality) played integral roles in the definition of the movement. Virginia Ramey Mollenkott contributed both in the historical development of the religious feminist position as well as to the ideological development. To introduce the need for a critical analysis of her thought, a brief overview of her life and theology is now offered as to the importance of such a work.

A PIONEER RELIGIOUS FEMINIST: VIRGINIA RAMEY MOLLENKOTT

Mollenkott viewed her encounter with early feminist ideas as life transforming. Developmentally and ideologically, Mollenkott was a catalytic influence on the development of religious feminism. A brief consideration of her background and contributions is now considered.

Her Brief Personal History

"When I was young, I memorized a lot of Scripture, all from the venerable King James version of 1611."[75] Mollenkott was born in Philadelphia, Pennsylvania, in 1932.[76] She grew up in a "fundamentalist" Plymouth Brethren home.[77] Although the culture and theology of that tradition did not allow divorce, her father left home when she was nine years old.[78] At some point during her adolescent years, Mollenkott had a relationship with an "older woman" that caused her mother to send her away to Christian high school.[79] In earlier books, Mollenkott did not divulge much detail about this relationship except to state that its nature was very alarming to her mother; however, in recent years Mollenkott revealed that it was a consensually sexual relationship.[80]

Mollenkott experienced being ostracized while away at school due to the warnings her mother gave the school administration about her involvement with the "older woman."[81] She recounted that eventually her roommates accepted her as a peer, although it took some time for them to include her in their activities. It was during this time that she memorized Scripture for comfort and decided to become a missionary.[82] Mollenkott went on to attend Bob Jones University to major in English.[83]

After graduating from college, Mollenkott married and became a mother.[84] She also went on to complete a Master of Arts degree in English and a Ph.D. from New York University. She described her marriage as an "attempt of a brainwashed fundamentalist to fit herself into the heteropatriarchal mold."[85] Her involvement in the biblical feminist movement began after her divorce from her husband of seventeen years.[86]

Mollenkott held teaching positions at Shelton College in Ringwood, New Jersey; Nyack Missionary College in Nyack, New York; and William Paterson College in Wayne, New Jersey. Currently, Mollenkott is Professor Emeritus at William Paterson University. She now resides with her life partner, Suzannah Tiltm, in New Jersey where she "co-grandmothers" her three grandchildren.[87]

Her Contribution to the Development of the Religious Feminist Movement

"Always an articulate and compelling speaker," Mollenkott gave the inaugural address at the first Evangelical Women's Caucus in Washington, DC, in 1975.[88] Her topic was on the need to "de-absolutize" cultural norms from patriarchal rule.[89] At that conference she also led workshops on "Models for Marriage" and "Woman to Woman Relationships." Both of these workshops laid foundations for later discussions on homosexuality within the EWC and became the early notes for her book *Women, Men and the Bible.*

Mollenkott published numerous books on central issues in the development of the biblical feminist movement. Her works include *Women, Men, & the Bible*; *Is the Homosexual My Neighbor?*; *Speech, Silence, Action*; *The Divine Feminine*; *Godding: Human Responsibility and the Bible*; *Omnigender: A Transreligious Approach*; and *Transgender Journeys.* Each one of these books represents an ideological contribution that influenced the organizational development of the group forward.

In June 1981, Mollenkott was invited to speak at the National Organization of Women's rally in Washington, DC, to support the Equal Rights Amendment.[90] As a representative of the Evangelical Women's Caucus and the National Council of Churches Religious Committee, she shared the podium with Alan Alda and NOW president Ellie Smith.[91] Mollenkott's physical presence gave the EWC national recognition.

From 1983–1985 Mollenkott joined the Committee for the Production of the Inclusive Language Lectionary for the National Council of Churches.[92] Her involvement in this process also signaled the movement in leadership of the EWC to issues of inclusive language and greater gender inclusiveness. At the split in the EWC at the 1986 Fresno conference, Mollenkott again gave the plenary address for the conference, wherein she insisted on the rejection of heterosexism.[93]

At each major developmental stage, the influence of Virginia Ramey Mollenkott was unmistakable. Her presence alone at such events is cause for more careful consideration. However, her authority is not only evidenced in the structure of the religious feminist movement, but also in her theoretical contributions.

Her Ideas on the Three Central Issues

Echoed in the development of the religious feminist movement, the life and thought of Virginia Ramey Mollenkott illustrated the concern and controversy over the three major issues debated in the movement. Each of her books, journal articles, and speeches dealt directly with the development of the theories of religious feminism. Mollenkott led the way in raising questions that the early feminists needed to consider, and throughout its development, she offered her opinions and ideas on the central concerns of biblical authority, hermeneutical methodology, and homosexuality.

Her first major theological work, *Women, Men, & the Bible*, introduced newer interpretations of biblical passages dealing with the roles of men and women. As an exegetical book, Mollenkott's ideas led the way in introducing the Christian feminist position according to the newer definition of biblical authority.[94] She also employed hermeneutical methods not traditionally accepted in the evangelical world. An example of these newer methods is found in her emphasis on culture as a tool for interpreting passages on gender roles in the Bible.[95] Mollenkott particularly noted the differences in the ancient Roman understanding of the term "head" as translated in 1 Corinthians 11 as different than the obvious meaning as the head of the body. She wrote, "But in biblical times, it was not known that the head makes the decisions and gives the orders to the nervous system. Decision-making was located in the heart, which is why we are told that our belief in Jesus is to take place in our hearts and that thoughts issue from the heart."[96] With the publication of *Women, Men, & the Bible* her emphasis shifted from scriptural authority alone to reason and experience. Her next book, *Is the Homosexual My Neighbor?*, also furthered the emphasis placed on reason, scientific evidence, and personal experience.

Mollenkott's theological movement is related to her opinion of biblical authority. In *Sensuous Spirituality*, she wrote, "Dreams were a part of the process that transformed me from a sense of my own total depravity to a sense that I am a spiritual being working for justice in a universe in which ultimately everything is alright."[97] Mollenkott's transitioned emphasis on her own experience rather than that of the authoritative nature of Scripture led her ultimately to moral inclusivism.[98]

When she joined the Committee for the Production of the Inclusive Language Lectionary for the National Council of Churches, Mollenkott advocated the acceptance of gender neutral religious resources. At the root of this practice was her belief and usage in newer hermeneutical practices. Using inclusive language was a step in the process of overthrowing the patriarchal rule of the church.[99] In *The Divine Feminine*, she advocated using inclusive language to refer to God.[100] She wrote, "It seems natural to assume that Christian people, eager to transmit the Good News that the Creator loves each human equally and unconditionally, would be right in the vanguard of those who utilize inclusive language."[101] Eventually, this usage led her to move from theism to panentheism.[102] Mollenkott's hermeneutical practice of inclusive language allowed for her theological movement as seen in the development in her thoughts through each of her books.

In an interview with Karin Granberg-Michealson, Mollenkott revealed that she thought she was "interested in same sex relationships when she was four years old."[103] She indicated in her writings that she always had a "lesbian voice;" however, she did not publicly identify her sexuality until 1987. Her support in favor of equal treatment and theological support of homosexuality spanned several decades. As Mollenkott's understanding of biblical authority moved and her emphasis on newer hermeneutical methods grew, her sexual identity was affected.

At each stage developmentally and ideologically, Virginia Ramey Mollenkott influenced the biblical feminist movement. Many religious feminists, and Mollenkott in particular, had the desire to transform evangelicalism with the message of equal treatment of women in the home, church, and society.[104] EWC archivist, S. Sue Horner noted their intentions, "Every feminist could act as a bridge between the secular feminist movement and those Christians who are fearful, misinformed, and afraid to take a new look at woman's role because they believe to do so is to go against Scripture."[105] These women (and some men) wanted to bring the message of religious feminism to all segments of the church, and Virginia Ramey Mollenkott greatly influenced their intentions.

Her Importance in the Women's Movement

Struggling to identify themselves in the era of the 1960s and 1970s, young evangelicals sought to be relevant during cultural crisis. Meeting the social needs of that day pressured leaders in many ways. Seeking to address cultural concerns pushed evangelical leaders in their traditional understandings of biblical authority and hermeneutical practices. The development of evangelical feminism came to exist in these circumstances. Social concerns for the equal treatment of women in the home, church, and society naturally fit into the concerns of young evangelicals. Understanding the history of religious feminism is contingent upon understanding the developments in the broader evangelical movement. One historian noted:

> The history of evangelical feminism is more than just a narrative of events. It also is a kind of 'color commentary' on the struggles over authority in American evangelicalism and religion more broadly and thus has important lessons to teach us about American evangelicalism, American religion generally, and the nexus between religion and public life.[106]

In theory and in practice, the development of the religious feminist movement exemplifies the struggles of evangelicalism in the past forty years. Understanding its primary developments and key issues sheds light on concerns within evangelicalism today. Within religious feminism, the question of biblical authority and acceptable hermeneutical practices led to an organizational and theological schism in 1986.[107] Issues present within that debate are still present within the evangelical feminist movement today.

As a leader in the religious feminist movement, Virginia Ramey Mollenkott is a pioneer. In fact, she sought not just to remain a member of evangelicalism but to transform it.[108] By staying within the bounds of evangelicalism with the usage of inclusive language, Mollenkott wishes to persuade other men and women through her ideas, and rejects the possibility that her theology is anything other than evangelical.[109] Understanding how Mollenkott holds such a view, though her life and theology contradict it, is the purpose of this book.

PURPOSE AND OVERVIEW

This book will analyze critically the religious feminist theology of Virginia Ramey Mollenkott. I argue that Mollenkott's life and theology exhibit a consistent move away from traditional evangelical Christianity due to cultural pressures and feminist presuppositions, though Mollenkott rejects such a movement. Following the discussion of Mollenkott's own feminist theological understanding, a critique is offered from a vantage within Mollenkott's own feminist model (internal critique) and from the vantage point of one who rejects Mollenkott's feminist theology (external critique).

The book is organized into chapters that deal with each portion of this analysis. Chapter 1 explains the need for such a study by offering a brief history of the religious feminist movement and a pioneer feminist, Virginia Ramey Mollenkott. Included in this introduction is a consideration of the need for such a work. Chapter 1 proposes that this book is needed based on her contributions to the field and because of what her theological move illustrates for others seeking to be culturally relevant in their theology.

Chapter 2 is a biographical sketch of Mollenkott. No major historical work exists at this point on the life of Virginia Mollenkott, so this chapter consists of her life as told through her books and interviews. Mollenkott refers to different phases of her life as representative of her theological status. These phases are chronicled in order to give a framework for understanding her theological shift in chapter 4.

An overview and summary of all twelve of her books makes up chapter 3. Books of particular interest in this thesis are *Women, Men, & the Bible*; *Is the Homosexual My Neighbor?*; *Godding*; and *The Divine Feminine*. Each book sheds light on Mollenkott's theological move based on the pressures of culture and feminist presuppositions. This chapter summarizes her scholarly contributions.

An analysis and organization of major themes in the construction of her theology composes chapter 4. Of particular interest in this analysis is the role of cultural pressure and feminist presuppositions in her development. Major theological themes that could be explored are the role of biblical authority and personal experience; the role of hermeneutical practices surrounding the use of inclusive language; and the progression of Mollenkott's theology towards universalism and away from traditional evangelical Christianity.

Chapter 5 concludes with an internal and external critique of her thought. First, a critique is proposed based on the logical acceptance of her thought. What problems and issues arise if one were to accept Mollenkott's theology? The external critique argues from the position of the outsider, or someone who does not accept Mollenkott's positions. The questions to be discussed are those that arise from outside her feminist presuppositions. Chapter 5 concludes with research implications of Mollenkott's theology and research applications of the critical analysis of her theology.

A work analyzing the progression of thought of one who lived during and attempted to respond to the women's movement through the eyes of her traditional faith is the task of this book. Virginia Mollenkott wanted to integrate feminist principles into her Christianity, hoping that her faith would remain truly evangelical Christian. However, evaluating if this desire was possible is the task of this book.

NOTES

1. Nancy Hardesty, *Women Called to Witness: Evangelical Feminism in the Nineteenth Century*, 2nd ed. (Knoxville: University of Tennessee Press, 1999), 138.

2. Pamela Cochran, *Evangelical Feminism: A History* (New York: New York University Press, 2005), 31.

3. Ibid., 15.

4. Sue S. Horner, *How Did EEWC Originate?* (Evangelical and Ecumenical Women's Caucus, 2001) [on-line]; accessed 19 February 2005; available from http://www.eewc.com/About.htm; Internet.

5. Sue S. Horner, "Becoming All We're Meant to Be: A Social History of the Contemporary Evangelical Feminist Movement, a Case Study of the Evangelical and Ecumenical Women's Caucus" (Ph.D. diss., Garrett-Evangelical Theological Seminary, 2000), 193.

6. Cochran, *Evangelical Feminism*, 2.

7. Ibid., 37.

8. Ibid.

9. Horner, *How Did EEWC Originate?*

10. Cochran, *Evangelical Feminism*, 37.

11. Ibid., 41.

12. Ibid., 70.

13. Hardesty, *Women Called to Witness*, 138.

14. Horner, "Becoming All We're Meant to Be," 215.

15. Ibid.

16. Ibid.

17. Ibid., 193.

18. Letha Scanzoni and Virginia R. Mollenkott, *Is the Homosexual My Neighbor?* (San Francisco: Harper & Row, 1978), ix.

19. Horner, "Becoming All We're Meant to Be," 193.

20. Ibid., 12.

21. Ibid., 3.

22. Cochran, *Evangelical Feminism*, 193.

23. Horner, "Becoming All We're Meant to Be," 193.

24. Cochran, *Evangelical Feminism*, 97.

25. Ibid., 193.

26. Ibid., 97.

27. Anne Eggebroten, "Handing Power," *The Other Side* (December 1986): 22.

28. Cochran, *Evangelical Feminism*. 96.

29. *Christians for Biblical Equality.*

30. Horner, *How Did EEWC Originate?*

31. Cochran, *Evangelical Feminism*, 186.

32. Ibid., 183.

33. *Christians for Biblical Equality* [on-line]; accessed 18 March 2005; available from http://www.cbeinternational.org; Internet.

34. Ibid.

35. See, "Christians for Biblical Equality: Who We Are," [on-line]; accessed 18 March 2005; available at http://www.cbeinternational.org/new/about/who_we_are.shtml; Internet.

36. Ibid.

37. Cochran, *Evangelical Feminism*, 111.

38. Ibid.

39. Ibid.

40. Kari Malcolm, "Who Will Be Real? When Will We Be Free?," *Priscilla Papers* 1, no. 1 (1987): 1.

41. Ibid.

42. Cochran, *Evangelical Feminism*, 190.

43. Cochran, *Evangelical Feminism*, 18.

44. Mary A. Kassian, *Women, Creation, and the Fall* (Wheaton, IL: Crossway, 1990), 209.

45. Scanzoni and Mollenkott, *Is the Homosexual My Neighbor?*, 130.

46. Virginia R. Mollenkott, *Sensuous Spirituality: Out from Fundamentalism* (New York: Crossroad, 1992), 16.

47. Cochran, *Evangelical Feminism*, 19–20.

48. Ibid.

49. Letha Scanzoni and Nancy Hardesty, *All We're Meant to Be: Biblical Feminism for Today*, rev. ed. (Nashville: Abingdon, 1986), 18.

50. Virginia R. Mollenkott, *Women, Men, & the Bible* (Nashville: Abingdon, 1977), 77.

51. Paul King Jewett, *Man as Male and Female: A Study in Sexual Relationships from a Theological Point of View* (Grand Rapids: Eerdmans, 1975), 134.

52. Mollenkott, *Women, Men, & the Bible*, 76.

53. Kassian, *The Feminist Gospel*, 58.

54. Cochran, *Evangelical Feminism*, 20.

55. Grant R. Osborne, *The Hermeneutical Spiral: A Comprehensive Introduction to Biblical Interpretation* (Downers Grove, IL: InterVarsity, 1991), 9–10.

56. Kassian, *The Feminist Gospel*, 209.

57. Ibid., 210.

58. Mollenkott, *Women, Men, & the Bible*, 74.

59. Ibid.

60. Kassian, *The Feminist Gospel*, 209.

61. Grudem, *Evangelical Feminism and Biblical Truth*, 377.

62. Cochran, *Evangelical Feminism*, 37.

63. Scanzoni and Hardesty, *All We're Meant to Be*, 231.

64. Simone DeBeauvoir, *The Second Sex* (New York: Random, 1989), 679.

65. Scanzoni and Mollenkott, *Is the Homosexual My Neighbor?*, 60.

66. Ibid., 55.

67. Don Williams, *The Bond That Breaks: Will Homosexuality Split the Church?* (Los Angeles: BIM, 1978), 46.

68. Horner, "Becoming All We're Meant to Be," 193.

69. Cochran, *Evangelical Feminism*, 90.

70. Kassian, *The Feminist Gospel*, 230.

71. Cochran, *Evangelical Feminism*, 77.

72. Virginia R. Mollenkott and Vanessa Sheridan, *Transgender Journeys* (Cleveland: Pilgrim, 2003), 123.

73. Kassian, *The Feminist Gospel*, 210.

74. Cochran, *Evangelical Feminism*, 106.

75. Mollenkott, *Sensuous Spirituality*, 15.

76. Mollenkott and Sheridan, *Transgender Journeys*, 41.

77. Karin Granberg-Michaelson, *We Are Who We Are by the Grace of God* [on-line]; accessed 14 March 2005; available from http://www.perspectivesjournal.org/2003/08/interview.php; Internet.

78. Mollenkott and Sheridan, *Transgender Journeys*, 41.

79. Granberg-Michaelson, *We Are Who We Are by the Grace of God*.

80. Ibid.

81. Mollenkott and Sheridan, *Transgender Journeys*, 42.

82. Ibid.

83. Granberg-Michaelson, *We Are Who We Are by the Grace of God*.

84. Virginia R. Mollenkott, *Speech, Silence, Action! The Cycle of Faith* (Nashville: Abingdon, 1980), 14.

85. Mollenkott, *Sensuous Spirituality*, 11–12.

86. Cochran, *Evangelical Feminism*, 53.

87. *Virginia Ramey Mollenkott* [online]; accessed 14 March 2005; available from http://www.geocities.com/vrmollenkott/?200514/; Internet.

88. Horner, "Becoming All We're Meant to Be," 195.

89. Cochran, *Evangelical Feminism,* 37.

90. Horner, "Becoming All We're Meant to Be," 195.

91. Cochran, *Evangelical Feminism*, 40.

92. Kassian, *The Feminist Gospel*, 237.

93. Cochran, *Evangelical Feminism*, 96.

94. Mollenkott, *Women, Men, & the Bible*, 71.

95. Ibid., 88.

96. Ibid., 92.

97. Mollenkott, *Sensuous Spirituality*, 27.

98. Kassian, *The Feminist Gospel*, 238.

99. Ibid.

100. Virginia R. Mollenkott, *The Divine Feminine: The Biblical Imagery of God as Female* (New York: Crossroad, 1983), 48.

101. Ibid., 1.

102. Ibid., 107.

103. Granberg-Michaelson, *We Are Who We Are by the Grace of God*.

104. Cochran, *Evangelical Feminism*, 58.

105. Horner, "Becoming All We're Meant to Be," 199.

106. Cochran, *Evangelical Feminism*, 3.

107. Ibid., 103.

108. Virginia R. Mollenkott, "Critical Inquiry and Biblical Inerrancy," *Religion and Public Education* (Winter 1990): 62.

109. Mollenkott, *Sensuous Spirituality*, 75.

Chapter Two

Biography

This chapter will consider the personal development of Mollenkott who cited this verse as a guiding principle for her life, "Brethren, I do not count myself to have apprehended; but one thing I do, forgetting those things which are behind and reaching forward to those things which are ahead, I press toward the goal for the upward call of God in Christ Jesus" (Phil 3:13–14). This quotation from the apostle Paul is insightful in understanding the life and theology of Virginia Ramey Mollenkott.

CHILDHOOD YEARS

Born in Philadelphia, Pennsylvania in 1932 to Plymouth Brethren parents, Virginia's childhood held many personal challenges.[1] Mollenkott rarely discussed details of her childhood except for how her upbringing contributed to her later development of ideas about her lesbianism and transgenderism. However, with regard to the actual events of her life, much can be observed from the few details she exposes.

"What I deeply appreciate from my own background is that I was thoroughly grounded in the surface facts (the words themselves) of the Bible. For that I feel grateful to my mother and to various brothers at the Plymouth Brethren Assemblies."[2] Though later in life Mollenkott differed greatly from her earlier Plymouth Brethren beliefs, she is always quick to give credit to this aspect of her childhood. It is interesting to note that in this tradition "women were not permitted to preach, or to pray aloud, or even to ask questions at the Bible 'readings.'"[3]

When Virginia was nine years old her father divorced her mother.[4] In an interview conducted in 2004, Mollenkott revealed that she observed patterns of abuse for generations in her family. However, when her father left her mother for another woman, the rest of the family moved to a poorer neighborhood in Philadelphia.

In the after effects of World War II, Virginia and her brother Bob experienced much racial tension in their new neighborhood. During these years Mollenkott recalled observing for the first time living conditions that were different from her own white, middle class upbringing. Her father left her mother with debt, so their financial well-being was disturbed as a result of the divorce. Her only friend during those years was a little girl named Mary Lou.[5] This friend lived across the driveway from the Ramey's, and Virginia regarded her as someone whom she would have "walked through fire for."[6] Later in life, Mollenkott identifies Mary Lou as one of her first same-sex attractions.

Throughout her early years, Virginia's struggle with obesity presented her with many challenges. For example, she was often compared to her brother who had no such weight problem, and he teased her about it. In later writings, Mollenkott says that his teasing caused her to identify with the "underdog" in arguments and eventually led to her concern for social justice.[7] She recounts listening to episodes of *The Lone Ranger*, with her brother enjoying candies and sweets, while she could have none of them.[8] For Mollenkott, these experiences as a young girl served to pave the road to her experiences of what she later calls her "oppression."

At age eleven, Mollenkott entered a relationship with a woman who was twenty-one.[9] She met this woman at her church, and was invited over to get to know her better.[10] Once there, the woman molested her; however, she does not recall it as a relationship of child abuse.[11] Mollenkott was convinced that she loved this woman, named Madeline, and that their relationship was consensual.[12] She identifies Madeline as the first person who ever loved her, therefore, her advances to young Mollenkott were welcomed. She wrote, "It felt wonderful to be loved and to love. But I hated it when I began to develop breasts, and slumped so badly trying to hide them that the family forced me to wear an extremely uncomfortable shoulder brace."[13] However, when her mother discovered her affair, she confronted Madeline's family and sent Virginia to a private boarding school in Florida called Hampden Dubose Academy.[14]

Before Virginia arrived at her new high school her mother told the administration of her relationship with Madeleine, and they in turn told the student body.[15] Virginia, according to the school's administration, was never to be left alone with other students. Contrary to her expectations, however, the students were relatively welcoming to her. It was the administration who gave her a difficult time throughout her experience there. She recounted in *Transgender Journeys*, written in 2003, that "periodically administrators told her that although there was no cure for her disease, nevertheless God had no use for her kind of person."[16] When she was thirteen, after months of enduring such treatment, she tried to kill herself.[17]

After her suicide attempt she was forced to stay in the school infirmary and required to read a book about the devil entitled *Whom Resist*. She was consistently told that God wanted nothing to do with people like her because of her lesbianism, yet she wrote that her desire to please Him stayed in tact. She wrote in *Is the Homosexual My Neighbor?*, her co-authored book with Letha Scanzoni, that she felt so dedicated to Christ that she "resolutely avoided" masturbation and other sexual expression during her teen years.[18] Her awareness of her lesbianism as a result of her relationship with Madeline awoke Virginia to her sexuality and her inability to express herself in the way that she felt most natural while still pleasing God. These frustrations only followed her into her college years.

COLLEGE YEARS

> When I was in high school and college, people used to assure me that I was trying too hard to be a good Christian. All I really had to do was 'let go and let God.' And I wanted to do exactly that. But let go of what? And let God do what? And how to let go? And how to let God? Nobody was very handy with the answers to those questions. In fact, I hardly dared frame the questions in my mind. They seemed impious and disrespectful. Anybody really spiritual wouldn't need to inquire.[19]

Virginia's personal growth and development continued to be shadowed by questions of her sexuality throughout her college years. After completing high school at Hampden Dubose Academy, Mollenkott enrolled in Bob Jones University in Greenville, South Carolina. In an interview conducted in September 2004, Virginia recalled attending there because it was where her mother could afford to support her financially and no other real educational alternatives occurred to her.[20]

Virginia's keen mind continued blossoming as she chose to study English literature while at Bob Jones. She recalled encountering a class on John Milton, the future subject of her doctoral dissertation, with great enthusiasm and interest. However, those years were also confusing for Virginia as she attempted to reconcile her growing intellectualism with her fundamentalist background. Often to Virginia, the two seemed to be diametrically opposed. While studying at Bob Jones University, often even popular conservative religious figures like Billy Graham were attacked as being too liberal.[21] The more Mollenkott grew in her intellectual abilities the more these kinds of statements were difficult for her to reconcile with her background.

Compounding her intellectual challenges was her confusion with regard to her sexuality. In her 1992 work, *Sensuous Spirituality*, Mollenkott wrote that she "sublimated" her sexuality throughout college with sports, studies and other good works.[22] She wrote of being "deeply dismayed" by the strict gender based rules at Bob Jones University. These rules included dress codes where women were required to wear nylon stockings all the time, even while playing tennis.[23] To Mollenkott, these rules signified a type of gender-based duplicity that was unacceptable.

She also recognized a double standard existing between those students who were heterosexual and those students who were homosexual. In *Omnigender*, Mollenkott's book published in 2001 in which she argues for a society that rejects the "binary gender construct" of males and females, she wrote that she "sensed" a culture on campus wherein if a person was popular with certain people of authority their alternate sexuality was accepted.[24] However, because Mollenkott never became friends with those authorities, she wrote that she "worked hard, lived celibate, earned top grades, and was invited to return to teach literature and write a daily radio program" after her graduation.[25]

Virginia guarded the secret of her lesbianism closely; however, she did share it with one trusted professor while studying at Bob Jones University.[26] When she told that professor that she was in love with another woman, the professor urged her to marry heterosexually.[27] By committing herself to a heterosexual relationship, the teacher instructed her that she would eventually fall in love with her husband and become a satisfied heterosexual.[28] Therefore, when Mollenkott was twenty-one years old she married Fred Mollenkott. She graduated that same year with her Bachelor of Arts in English Literature from Bob Jones University.[29]

Once her undergraduate work was completed, Mollenkott, newly married, pursued her Master's degree from Temple University and her Doctor of Philosophy in English Literature from New York University. Her consistent personal and intellectual development did not match her fundamentalist beliefs from her childhood. As she grew in her understanding in the academy, her personal religious beliefs were increasingly challenged. Details of her life during her graduate and doctoral work are considered next in this biography.

GRADUATE AND EARLY PROFESSIONAL YEARS

Mollenkott often recalled difficulties she encountered while completing her education. She wrote:

> I remember the health-wrecking tension of those Ph.D. years: teaching full time and chairing the English department at Shelton College, taking care of a small son

and being responsible for the washing, ironing, bed making, cleaning, shopping, cooking—the works. I remember feeling it was unfair that my husband could get up from dinner and watch TV all evening while I washed the dishes, put the baby to bed, and then cleared a place for myself on the kitchen table to study for my graduate courses and prepare for my next day's classes. I frequently worked until the wee hours, always struggling to shut out the sound of the incessant television.[30]

In *Sensuous Spirituality*, she called her marriage to Fred Mollenkott, "the attempt of a brainwashed fundamentalist to fit herself into the heteropatriarchal mold."[31] Even facing these pressures and struggles in her marriage, Mollenkott pursued her graduate education and excelled in it. Her doctoral dissertation entitled *Milton and the Apocrypha* won the Andiron Award from NYU in 1964 for the best doctoral dissertation in English.[32]

It was Milton's opinions that affected her thinking on Christians seeking divorce.[33] She wrote, "From Milton I learned how to read the Bible in a liberating way."[34] Therefore, as she studied alternative ways to interpret the Bible from Milton and other newer theologians, her traditional faith heritage seemed less believable.[35] She wrote in her 1980 book *Speech, Silence, Action!*, where she details her spiritual progression, "So, for those of you who wonder where I was during the worst of the 1960s when you needed all the help you could get, the answer is that I was sorting through my fundamentalist heritage and otherwise very busy surviving."[36] During the 1950s and 1960s Mollenkott was finishing her education and trying to survive her marriage to Fred Mollenkott.

Her development intellectually parallels her growth away from her fundamentalist religious beliefs. She simultaneously experienced difficulty in her marriage and success and prestige in the academic world. While finishing her education she chaired English departments at Shelton College in New Jersey and Nyack Missionary College in New York.[37] Winning the academic award for best dissertation and chairing English departments were accomplishments that only seemed to fuel Mollenkott's growing disagreement with her fundamentalist beliefs.

Commenting on the anti-intellectual climate of her fundamentalist background, Mollenkott wrote:

> Worship of the intellect (from outside fundamentalism) has led to deep-seated, demoralizing distrust of it [among fundamentalists]. While I was teaching in fundamentalist or evangelical colleges (until 1967), through discussion of great literature I tried to demonstrate the difference between mere emotionalism (pietistic or otherwise) and genuine emotion (always closely integrated with rational thought and clear perception).[38]

Exposure to intellectual stimulation while striving to meet the marital expectations of her husband, and teaching fairly at Nyack Missionary College and

Shelton College proved too much pressure for Mollenkott. She recalled viewing her entire doctoral process as a game, telling herself that all she had to do was complete each requirement one at a time.[39] That way, she could focus on only what was required from her next.

In her own classroom, Mollenkott "followed a rigid policy of returning all . . . papers from the five separate courses she was teaching, graded with comments, within one week of the time she received them so that the students would not have time to lose interest in their results."[40] Her high expectations of herself met with displeasure from her husband. As difficult as her academic successes were to attain, they contributed to her growing sense of achievement while her satisfaction in her wifely role lessened.

In an explanation of the reason for her eventual divorce in 1967, Mollenkott wrote, "Still, there was the atmosphere at home, where my husband assured me that all troubles in our marriage were the result of my own childishness. Mature women, particularly if they believed God's word, had no difficulty with their subordinate role in church and home."[41] Five years after her marriage to Fred Mollenkott, Virginia gave birth to a son, Paul, "hoping against hope that it would somehow improve our marriage."[42] Soon, however, Virginia realized that her son, while she loved and enjoyed being a mother, was not the solution to her marital dissatisfaction.[43]

> When the Ph.D. was completed, I faced other pressures that I had been postponing. Like the fact that my marriage was hopeless. Like that fact that I was extremely lonely and starved for emotional support. Like the fact that my health was poor. In 1967, suspecting that some day I might have to get a divorce and sensing that the job market might tighten, I left Nyack for the state college where I still teach.[44]

By this time her exposure to John Milton's ideas on divorce and other sources has convinced Mollenkott that she must separate from her husband. Therefore, after seventeen years of marriage, Virginia Ramey Mollenkott ended this period of her life, beginning her radical evolution in feminist and later lesbian-bisexual-gay-transgender thought.[45]

EARLY ADULT YEARS: 1967–EARLY 1980s

The year of 1967 was an eventful year for Virginia Ramey Mollenkott. She quit her teaching position at Nyack Missionary College, formally ending her affiliation with fundamentalist schools; took another teaching position at Paterson State College in New Jersey; divorced her husband; and published her first book, *Adamant and Stone Chips*. Her personal development can best be observed from the evolution of her thought in her books. This section, therefore, will chronicle her life as revealed through the books she published from 1967–1980.

The Year 1967

In Mollenkott's first published book, *Adamant and Stone Chips*, she deals with her theological leanings as a Christian humanist.[46] In this way, Mollenkott wrote honestly about her attempt to reconcile her spiritual background in fundamentalism with her continued growth in the intellectual academy. She defines a Christian humanist as one who:

> Takes the positive approach to academics, aesthetics, and human relationships. He maintains that in spite of the radical dislocations brought about by the fall of man, Christ remains the King of all creation both through His creatorial powers and through His redemptions. The Christian humanist seeks for truth in the works of man, knowing that the rain falls both on just and unjust and that (for reasons man cannot really assess) God often chooses apparently unregenerate minds to reveal fragments of His glory to us. The Christian humanist recognizes no fragmentization or compartmentalization in the life of a committed Christian.[47]

She recognized that her background invoked a fear of knowledge apart from a literal reading of the Bible and salvation in Christ.[48] Her thoughts in this book reveal the Mollenkott who is searching for her identity as an intelligent woman of faith.

The Years 1969–1976

In Search of Balance was published in 1969 by Mollenkott and in it she revealed more of her journey to reconcile her faith with her educational vocation. She wrote, "I had lived without balance because I had not really known who I was. . . . I had achieved a Ph.D., and on the surface I looked anything but indecisive. My lack of balance stemmed from a tacitly assumed concept of God which had turned me into a drifter."[49] In this quote Mollenkott disclosed her continuing attempt to reconcile the two major parts of her life. She also wrote, "Like many brought up in the evangelical tradition, I had assumed that Christ was that organizing hub and that no further thinking was necessary. But lately I began to wonder whether Christ ever intended to be as passive as I had been? Had He wanted His followers to be the mere victims of fate?"[50] The tension between her fundamentalist beliefs and her educational passions seemed to build with each achievement of Mollenkott.

Another issue for Mollenkott from *In Search of Balance* was her continuing search for her identity. Was she simply the sum of other people's opinions or was she whom she believed inside that she was? These questions, for Mollenkott, surround questions of her sexuality, yet only later in her writing did she identify them as such. She wrote, "I knew then and know now that I can't live my whole life trying to please other people; but on what basis do I decide when to go my own way or which way really IS my own?"[51] She continued, "And does living for others mean sacrificing my plans to theirs, my desires to theirs, my whole identity to theirs? Isn't this just about the most direct route to a whopping neurosis?"[52] Her search for wholeness was beginning to push her past her fundamentalism. Trite sayings that she grew up hearing as the way to live Christianly were no longer authoritative for Virginia as she grew in her early adult years.

This early tendency is also noticeable in her writing. She wrote, "I recognize that if an individual rejects all authority, he sets himself adrift at the mercy of his own whims—and may soon find himself at the mercy of the whims of men more powerful than himself."[53] The struggle for authority in the life of Virginia Ramey Mollenkott would play a vital role in her evolving theology through the next several decades. In the above quote, she revealed her early position to depend solely on the authority of the Bible, however, this tendency changed in later years.

The Years 1977–1979

> By the early 1970s the books I was choosing to read were more and more centered on issues of justice. . . . Not long thereafter, I began to be sensitized about justice for women, and since then have been engaged in various justice-causes that seem an authentic response to the "still, small voice" within my nature.[54]

The influence of this new reading list proved to change the course of Virginia's life. Through the emphasis on social justice, Virginia for the first time encountered thought on feminism and liberation theology. From this material came her growing conviction that her Christianity could be united with her new beliefs in feminism. Therefore, in 1977 Virginia published *Women, Men, & the Bible* through Abingdon Press.

In this book, Mollenkott argued, for the first time, her position on the Bible's liberating message for women. By this time Virginia had become convinced that the teachings of her early fundamentalist years were incorrect, and this work clearly stated her move away from allegiance to them. In later revisions of her next book published first in 1978, *Is the Homosexual My Neighbor?* Mollenkott revealed that she confessed her lesbianism to her friend and co-author Letha Scanzoni in 1975.[55] So, for better or for worse,

Mollenkott's thought as developed in *Women, Men, & the Bible* and *Is the Homosexual My Neighbor?* set her on a course to be explored personally and professionally for the next three decades.

The Year 1980

"My development during approximately the past 15 years has, in one sense, been a development away from an almost entire focus on words, books, and ideas (speech), through a time of learning about silence, and finally into the field of action."[56] Published in 1980, Mollenkott's next book, *Speech, Silence, Action!*, candidly discussed several key issues. She wrote, "It is difficult for people who have not known a fundamentalist background to believe the basic, almost primitive struggles such a background can generate in fundamentalist persons as they become educated."[57] Her continuing endeavor to break free from her fundamentalist background shadowed her thoughts as discussed in this book.

Mollenkott discussed her crisis in trying to find her place within evangelicalism. She wrote that she felt "destined to be forever marginal: too radical for most evangelicals, too addicted to the Bible for many people in the mainline churches."[58] Yet, she attempted to unite both her beliefs in the Bible and feminism. She encouraged other ecumenists to read the Bible as the "liberating" work that it was, especially in the attempt to promote "an all-inclusive, global vision of human justice, dignity, and oneness."[59]

Furthermore, Mollenkott's contributions to the Evangelical Women's Caucus drew national attention for the group. In June 1981, Mollenkott was invited to speak at the National Organization of Women's rally in Washington, DC to support the Equal Rights Amendment.[60] As a representative of the Evangelical Women's Caucus and the National Council of Churches Religious Committee, she shared the podium with Alan Alda and NOW president Ellie Smith.[61] Her involvement with these organizations furthered the outside influences contributing to Mollenkott's ideological movement which increased significantly in years following her appearances.

LATER ADULT YEARS: 1983–PRESENT

The year 1983 brought the publication of her first book dealing specifically with inclusive language, *The Divine Feminine*. In this work Mollenkott introduced several new ideas for considering female imagery of God in the Bible. As her thought progressed in uniting Christianity and feminism, so did her desire to re-symbolize Christianity through the use of inclusive gender language. Specific life circumstances are not provided in the book; however, the expansion in her thought is important in this chronology of her life.

The Years 1987–2000

In 1987, Mollenkott published *Godding: Human Responsibility and the Bible.*
In this work Mollenkott discussed her spiritual growth in increasingly universal terms. She wrote of one such experience, "Not long ago, feeling very
afraid of my own inner process, I tried to circumvent my conscious mind
and to get in touch with my deeper awareness by asking the *I Ching* what
attitude I should take in my current difficulties. The hexagram I received was
29, the Abysmal (water)."[62] She credits much of her growth during the 1980s
to her involvement in the Women of Faith in Dialogue project. This work
was a group of women from different religious backgrounds contributing to
ecumenical understanding of women's work during that decade. During these
interactions, Mollenkott also came into contact with women of varying backgrounds and beliefs, in which the goal was to find common ground of beliefs
for continuing the liberation of women.[63]

With her publication of *Sensuous Spirituality*, Mollenkott further expressed her theological movement through her personal commitments and her
spiritual experiences. She wrote in this book:

> Like Carter Heyward, I speak and always have spoken in a lesbian voice; the
> feminism came much later than the lesbianism, signs of which were apparent in
> me by age four. Although I have come to identify myself essentially as a spiri-
> tual being who is currently having embodied human experiences, those experi-
> ences have been authentically lesbian for as long as I can remember.[64]

Two pages later she expressed her "profound gratitude" to her partner, Debra
Lynn Morrison.[65] She also includes an interesting discussion as to the reasons
for her movement in this book.

> Here I want only to explain why I myself switched from the traditional herme-
> neutics I have outlined here. In the first place, as a woman (and a lesbian at
> that) I was desperate. Like the Greek woman who became creative and assertive
> because she was desperate for the healing of her daughter, I was desperate for
> authenticity, for the healing of my self esteem, and for the use of my gifts.[66]

This candid confession by Mollenkott for the reason motivating her theological move is vital for understanding her life and her theology. Throughout
Mollenkott's life her attempt to make sense of her difficult childhood experiences, her sexual identity, and her religious beliefs drove her to move theologically. She later wrote that her definition of "Christian humanist" changed
through the years to being one who makes it "possible for everybody to feel
fully alive."[67]

There is a key distinction here from her earlier concern that every person understands *being* fully alive from everyone *feeling* fully alive. She later identified the Bible as the source of her "liberation," and wished "that every les-bi-gay person could know for herself the kind of empowerment and sense of community that coming out has afforded," to her, she continued, "Even my reading of the Bible has been invigorated."[68] By this time in Mollenkott's life, her theology and her personal integrity were defined more based on her new hermeneutical readings of the Bible and outside influences from other spiritual sources.

The Years 2001–Present

By the time of the publication of her final two books, Virginia Ramey Mollenkott had moved far away from her fundamentalist roots and early evangelical leanings. In 2001, she published *Omnigender*, wherein she argued for a society based on gender as individually defined, formally rejecting any traditional understanding of humanity as male and female. She wrote of herself, "I can now acknowledge that to the degree I feel myself to be a masculine woman, I am transgendered. Not transsexual. I feel myself to be female, alright, but masculine at the same time, so that dresses and skirts feel rather ridiculous—and this despite the fact that as a child I was not allowed to wear overalls, shorts, and pants."[69]

Mollenkott, in these final two books, revealed that she believed there was no such thing as "gender normality," and that each person should be able to choose what aspects of maleness or femaleness one desired to express.[70] In fact, she wrote, "I was sixty-four years old before I became fully conscious of the fact that I am a masculine woman, and that the deepest oppression I have known stemmed not simply from being female, nor even from being lesbian, but from being a gender transgressor."[71] Her movement as begun in 1977 for the liberation of women, moved effectually to liberation of homosexual people, finally to the need to redefine all gender constructs.

Her final book, *Transgender Journeys*, co-authored with Vanessa Sheridan, a male-to-female cross dresser, encouraged people of all types of gender identity to come out and join the endeavor to become the "new humanity." By this time, Mollenkott had fully moved from traditionally accepted evangelical morality, while still proclaiming to be evangelical.

Near the conclusion of her last work, Mollenkott again credited the Bible as her "radicalizer."[72] She discussed the dissenting role that her religious background afforded her in her personal and theological development. She wrote that her Plymouth Brethren background was both "oppressive and liberating."[73] Expressed this way:

Although she learned exceedingly negative biblical interpretations concerning women's gender roles and the status of homosexuals and other transgenderists, nevertheless she was grounded in a solid knowledge of biblical narratives and principles. That knowledge sprang into new significance when she learned a liberating method of interpreting Scripture, her primary role model being the seventeenth century Puritan poet and theologian, John Milton.[74]

Currently, Virginia Ramey Mollenkott resides in New Jersey with her life partner, Suzannah Tilton. After forty-four years of teaching she retired on February 1, 1997, and now holds the title of Professor Emeritus in English at William Paterson University of New Jersey. To date, *Transgender Journeys* is Mollenkott's last published work.

CONCLUSION

Virginia Ramey Mollenkott experienced in her earlier life many painful experiences that overshadowed her adult theological and personal development. Her early exposure to the fundamentalist Plymouth Brethren tradition gave her a foundation of believing in the Bible. However, as she went through painful experiences with her family, that same tradition failed her in aiding her understanding and interpretation of those events. Therefore, Virginia spent much time throughout her adult years trying to make sense of her early experiences.

Additionally, as she encountered various reference materials on spirituality and natural science, her early faith was not intellectually mature enough to meet with the questions and challenges she met in her educational career. This occurrence further fueled Mollenkott's journey away from traditional orthodoxy in an attempt to understand herself and her pain.

In the following chapters, the development of her specific thought concerning her theology and ministry emphasis will be discussed and then analyzed. However, this portion of the critical analysis of the feminist theology of Virginia Ramey Mollenkott has purposed to provide the framework of life experiences from which her ideological movement occurred.

NOTES

1. It is important to note here the nature of the Plymouth Brethren religious community in which Mollenkott grew up. While the Plymouth Brethren tradition is a part of the evangelical community, it is also fundamentalist in nature. This term means that they had a strong commitment to being "militant in opposition to liberal theology in the churches . . . and cultural mores." George Marsden, *Understanding Fundamentalism and Evangelicalism* (Grand Rapids: William B. Eerdmans, 1991), 1. Marsden

goes on to note that fundamentalists are evangelicals who are "angry about something" and willing to fight about it. This understanding should be held in distinction with the rest of the evangelical community which would not necessarily be joined in a fight against liberalism. However, a distinction between fundamentalism and evangelicalism is important in understanding the situation in which Mollenkott grew up.

2. Ibid., 22.

3. Ibid.

4. Doris Malkmus, *Lgbtran-Oral History Project* (Religious Archives Network, 24 September 2004) [on-line]; accessed 13 June 2005; available from http://www.lgbtran.org/Exhibits/Mollenkott/ Bio.htm; Internet.

5. Virginia R. Mollenkott and Vanessa Sheridan, *Transgender Journeys* (Cleveland: Pilgrim, 2003), 41.

6. Ibid.

7. Mollenkott, *Speech, Silence, Action!*, 41.

8. Ibid.

9. Mollenkott and Sheridan, *Transgender Journeys*, 42.

10. Malkmus, *Lgbtran-Oral History Project*.

11. Mollenkott and Sheridan, *Transgender Journeys*, 42.

12. Malkmus, *Lgbtran-Oral History Project*.

13. Mollenkott and Sheridan, *Transgender Journeys*, 42.

14. Malkmus, *Lgbtran-Oral History Project*.

15. Ibid.

16. Ibid.

17. Virginia R. Mollenkott, *Omnigender: A Trans-Religious Approach* (Cleveland: Pilgrim, 2001), 124.

18. Letha Scanzoni and Virginia Mollenkott, *Is the Homosexual My Neighbor? Another Christian View* (San Francisco: Harper and Row, 1978), 104.

19. Virginia R. Mollenkott, *In Search of Balance* (Waco, TX: Word, 1969), 30.

20. Malkmus, *Lgbtran Oral History Project*.

21. Mollenkott, *Speech, Silence, Action!*, 20.

22. Virginia R. Mollenkott, *Sensuous Spirituality: Out from Fundamentalism* (New York: Crossroad, 1992), 161.

23. Mollenkott, *Omnigender*, 43.

24. Ibid.

25. Ibid.

26. Mollenkott, *Sensuous Spirituality*, 161.

27. Ibid.

28. Ibid.

29. Malkmus, *Lgbtran Oral History Project*.

30. Mollenkott, *Speech, Silence, Action!*, 18.

31. Mollenkott, *Sensuous Spirituality*, 12.

32. Mollenkott, *In Search of Balance*, i.

33. Mollenkott and Sheridan, *Transgender Journeys*, 45.

34. Ibid.

35. Mollenkott, *Speech, Silence, Action!*, 21.

36. Ibid.

37. Ibid.

38. Ibid., 32.

39. Ibid., 18–19.

40. Ibid., 19.

41. Ibid., 20.

42. Mollenkott and Sheridan, *Transgender Journeys*, 44.

43. Ibid., 19.

44. Mollenkott, *Speech, Silence, Action!*, 19–20.

45. Malkmus, *Lgbtran Oral History Project*.

46. Virginia R. Mollenkott, *Adamant & Stone Chips: A Christian Humanist Approach to Knowledge* (Waco, TX: Word, 1968), 7.

47. Ibid., 29.

48. Ibid., 12.

49. Ibid., 13.

50. Ibid., 15.

51. Ibid., 16.

52. Ibid., 27.

53. Ibid., 32.

54. Ibid., 40.

55. Scanzoni and Mollenkott, *Is the Homosexual My Neighbor?*, vii.

56. Mollenkott, *Speech, Silence, Action!*, 22.

57. Ibid.

58. Ibid., 25.

59. Ibid., 27.

60. Sue S. Horner, "Becoming All We're Meant to Be: A Social History of the Contemporary Evangelical Feminist Movement, a Case Study of the Evangelical and Ecumenical Women's Caucus," (Ph.D. diss., Garrett-Evangelical Theological Seminary, 2000), 195.

61. Pamela Cochran, *Evangelical Feminism: A History* (New York: New York University Press, 2005), 40.

62. Virginia R. Mollenkott, *Godding: Human Responsibility and the Bible* (New York: Crossroad, 1987), 134.

63. Virginia R. Mollenkott, "Critical Inquiry and Biblical Inerrancy," *Religion and Public Education* (winter 1990): 63.

64. Mollenkott, *Sensuous Spirituality*, 11.

65. Ibid., 13.

66. Ibid., 68.

67. Ibid., 72.

68. Ibid., 161–62.

69. Mollenkott, *Omnigender*, ix.

70. Ibid.

71. Ibid., 38.

72. Ibid., 99.

73. Ibid.

74. Ibid.

Chapter Three

Summary of the Books of Virginia Ramey Mollenkott

With her first publication in 1967, Mollenkott identified herself as a Christian humanist. The ideas included in that book, *Adamant and Stone Chips*, serve as a seedbed for the development of her thoughts in the following years. This chapter summarizes several of her significant books with the view of analyzing her works in later chapters.

ADAMANT AND STONE CHIPS

In her first published book, Virginia Ramey Mollenkott concerned herself more with the understanding of what it meant to be an intelligent Christian than with ideas she would later develop regarding feminist theology. *Adamant and Stone Chips* presented her view of Christian humanism and the cultural need for its acceptance.

She wrote, "Christian humanism subordinates the human to the divine because of the creature's proper relationship to the Creator."[1] She went on to express the concern that in her experience there seemed to be a fear of knowledge in Christianity at the time of her writing. Mollenkott, as evidenced in later writings, is here attempting to reconcile her early experiences with Christianity and her academic achievements.

She wrote regarding this observation of the Christian world and academia:

The Christian pursues knowledge in the realization that every academic area revolves around Him, the hub of the universe and therefore the university. The Christian student with a unified vision knows that the more he learns about the universe, the more fully and intelligently he will be able to worship the Maker of it all.

33

The "unified vision" of the universe Mollenkott mentioned is one wherein an understanding of reality includes both a concept of God as "Divine Maker" and man as made in His image, and nothing less. She wrote, "To a person with an eye single for God's glory, to a person who understands the New Testament principle that everything in life may be and should be done to the glory of God, to the person with a unified vision, God is not restricted to certain categories but is truly omnipresent."[2] Therefore, the appreciation of each moment and every aspect and person of it is mandatory.

Specifically, this line of thought finds expression, for the Christian humanist, in 1 Corinthians 13. Love for other people and love for God is the hub around which everything should surround, according to Christian humanism.[3] Human relationships become the test for loving God.[4] Faith has a role to play in the human economy of relationships, and love is the goal and motivator. For Mollenkott, this idea in its seedbed form here, informs her thoughts through the next several decades.

The main ideological thrust of the book is found on page forty-one and in the last chapter. She wrote:

> Doubtless it is fear of such progression which has motivated the obscurantism of many twentieth century evangelicals. If we give an inch to human reason, the argument goes, it will take a mile. If we open our minds to liberal education, we will lose our moorings and become doctrinally so liberal as to be lost to Christ's cause; therefore we will make a wholesale repudiation of culture and will withdraw into a special communion of the saints which is isolated from involvement with contemporary society. We will not read contemporary authors or defile ourselves with contemporary art forms; we will be assured that we will not fall prey to a creeping secularization. But the fallacy is, of course, that it is impossible to isolate oneself completely from the century into which God has placed us, and if it were possible it would not be advisable or Scriptural. Furthermore, the repudiation of the highest forms of human culture often leads to a creeping secularism of the basest sort; instead of falling prey to secularistic enjoyment of fine music an art and literature, the isolationist all too often falls prey to gross materialism and moral insensitivity.[5]

This type of thinking followed Mollenkott into much of her work in the social realm in years following her writing it. The need for the divine relationship with God to play out practically in the human realm is the framework from which Mollenkott wrote. She began her writing career in *Adamant and Stone Chips* by introducing her thoughts based on an appreciation of all that is Christian: God, the Bible, love, forgiveness, truth; with all that is human: relationships, pain, art, and literature. This then, is Christian humanism, and the first book by Virginia Ramey Mollenkott.

IN SEARCH OF BALANCE

Her second published book, *In Search of Balance*, was largely an autobiographical sketch of her journey outside of her fundamentalist background and into a more informed faith. As the name of the book denoted, her journey to find a balance in her Christianity is expressed in this book.

Personal fulfillment and satisfaction, for Mollenkott, was the focus of her life for many years. She wrote:

> I had lived without balance because I had not really known who I was. . . . I had achieved a Ph.D., and on the surface I looked anything but indecisive. My lack of balance stemmed from a tacitly assumed concept of God which had turned me into a drifter.[6]

The "tacitly assumed concept of God" referred to her fundamentalist upbringing where she learned to assume many things about God, like understanding God's will.[7] She wrote, "Like many brought up in my evangelical tradition, I had assumed that Christ was that organizing hub and that no further thinking was necessary. But lately I began to wonder whether Christ ever intended man to be as passive as I had been; had he wanted His followers to be the mere victims of fate?"[8]

Consequently, Mollenkott dealt with her understanding of authority in this book. Part of her Plymouth Brethren background would have included a very strict concept of authority. In this book, Mollenkott did not stray very far from that understanding. Her ideas were evident in thoughts such as, "One gains freedom through meaningful voluntary limitation. It's paradoxical. It's self contradictory. In a way it's absurd. But it's true."[9] In her later writings, her questioning of authority became more central.

She concluded the book by offering several examples of paradox. She included in these the paradox of the Trinity, the paradox of the Incarnation, the paradox of the nature of man and man's depravity and his righteousness.[10] All of these doctrines would continue to be important themes in her later books. Her final thought, however, is poignant:

> As I exercise my privilege of interpreting Scripture, it is essential that I open my mind to both poles of paradoxical truths, teaching them and living in awareness of them, so that my vision may survive reference to the complexities and contradictions of experience. This commits me, I know, to a continual search for a continually shifting balance. And search I will.[11]

As this overview of her books continues, it is interesting to take note of how this open mindedness Mollenkott wrote of in 1969 led her in later years.

WOMEN, MEN, & THE BIBLE

The first major theological contribution from Virginia Ramey Mollenkott came in 1977 with the publication of *Women, Men, & the Bible*. This work was one of the earliest attempts to harmonize secular feminist ideology with Christianity. The thesis of this book was, "*Women, Men, & the Bible* targets patriarchalism as a Christian heresy and hence necessarily interprets the whole Bible from a Christian perspective."[12] This overview is divided into four sections: The Christian vs. The Patriarchal Way of Relating, Imagery and Language Use in the Bible, Biblical Interpretation, and Major Bible Doctrines and Equality. Each section represents chapters dealing with the respective topics.

The Christian vs. the Patriarchal Way of Relating

"It is my assumption that if we are interested in understanding the Christian way of relating to others, the Bible must be our central source, and the teachings and behavior of Jesus must provide our major standard of judgment."[13] According to Mollenkott, the entire question of manhood and womanhood comes down to an understanding of how human beings relate to each other. Therefore, the first two chapters of *Women, Men, & the Bible* focused on this question.

Mollenkott began with the way that Jesus related to women and compared his treatment of women with the treatment they would have received according to the general cultural mores of the day.[14] She lists several indications of the poor treatment of women in Jesus day. Among these are easy access to divorce for men, higher blessing for the birth of boys over girls, and societal respect for women only through marriage and motherhood.[15]

Conversely, Mollenkott detailed Jesus' treatment of women with the highest of dignity and respect. She lists his encounter in Matthew 9 with the woman who had the issue of blood and the woman caught in adultery in John 8 as examples of how Jesus treated women in this manner. She also stated that Jesus redefined womanhood, however, in Luke 11:27 when he responded to a woman who shouted at him, "Happy the womb that carried you and the breasts that suckled you" (Luke 11:27 NEB)! Mollenkott understood this quote to mean that Jesus' definition of womanhood meant, "For women as well as for men, biology is not destiny. Rather, spiritual commitment is destiny."[16]

Early on, Mollenkott introduced a major term for the development of her thought. She wrote, "Even Jesus' own disciples failed to grasp his repeated teaching that the Christian way of relating is mutual submission and mutual service."[17] At this point, the central idea of Mollenkott's early feminist theology was revealed. She went on to write that both Paul and Peter taught mutual service and submission. For Paul she quoted Galatians 5:3 and Romans 12:10, specifically relating this concept to gender roles according to 1 Corinthians 16:16 where Paul wrote, "that you also submit to such, and to everyone who works and labors with us."

Her critique of patriarchy found expression mainly through reaction to several popular books in the 1970s. Among these are Marabel Morgan's *The Total Woman* and Judith M. Miles book, *The Feminine Principle: A Woman's Discovery of the Key to Total Fulfillment.*[18] Her critique focused on the views of these authors regarding hierarchal marriage relationships and denial of female humanity based on roles of wife and mother.[19] In this way, Mollenkott's argument against patriarchy ran parallel to secular feminist critique of popular culture in her time.

Imagery and Language Use in the Bible

> During the last several years, radical feminists have been saying that if God is male, then male is God. I had very little sympathy for such statements until I began to read the various attacks on equal-partnership marriage which were discussed in chapter 2. Reading them, I have been forced to realize that the exclusive use of male pronouns concerning God, the association of God with masculinity to the exclusion of femininity, has indeed been the cause of much idolatry.[20]

With these words Mollenkott moved into her analysis of the need for more feminine God language. She did not support feminine language over masculine language, but a combination of the two. She wrote that using masculine God language over feminine language was damaging for two reasons. First, it was damaging because it caused Christians to ignore all the feminine references to God, and second, because it caused Christians to refer to God only in the masculine without even acknowledging that there was any possibility of feminine language use to refer to God.[21]

Mollenkott argued that an entire revision of the Christian understanding of the Trinity was necessary.[22] She stated that since in Genesis 1:26 mankind was created "male and female in the image of God" that God, therefore, must be both male and female in order for humans to be in his/her image.[23] She cited the incarnation of Jesus, also, in support of her thesis. Because during his incarnation Jesus submitted to the Father, Mollenkott reasoned that He was exemplifying what at that time was a feminine role.[24] Therefore, Jesus spoke of himself in both masculine and feminine terms. She wrote:

> The combining of the typical Hebrew masculine and feminine sex-role characteristics in the person of Jesus created a beautiful picture of him as the embodiment

of all humanity, both male and female, who is then perfectly equipped to redeem the sins of us all, both male and female.[25]

She further developed her argument for masculine and feminine language for God based on the metaphor of the dove for the Holy Spirit.[26] She noted that because the dove is an androgynous symbol, combining both male and female aspects, the Spirit also represents male and female characteristics. She concluded that since according to Scripture there are aspects both of masculinity and femininity in the Godhead, Christian language should reflect it as well. However, Mollenkott argued that much of the hindrance to using feminine language for God rests on incorrect stereotypes, therefore her argument focused on the origin of stereotypes next.[27]

Mollenkott cited traditional stereotypes of boys and girls as inadequate based on sociological and psychological evidence.[28] She supported her claim based on several studies done in different cultures and places. Studies done by Margaret Mead were among the most quoted by Mollenkott.[29] Mead, an anthropologist, found that in tribes in New Guinea men and women had much different ideal temperaments.[30] This finding, for Mollenkott, supported her idea that socialization is principally cultural and not biblically based.

Biblical Interpretation

Before Mollenkott addressed any hermeneutical questions, she first dealt with interpretation questions related to the Apostle Paul and his letters. Here, for the first time, Mollenkott introduced her idea of the "absolutization" of culture.[31] She wrote:

> Many of the Old Testament authors assume that patriarchy is the will of God for the social order; in other words, they assume that men should have absolute power over their families, over worship, and over society in general. In the New Testament the same patriarchal assumption prevails, with several notable exceptions: Jesus' personal behavior, the passages concerning mutual submission, and several prophetic passages which envision the regenerative effects of the gospel on human society. Because patriarchy is the culture background of the Scriptures, it is absolutely basic to any feminist reading of the Bible that one cannot absolutize the culture in which the Bible was written.[32]

Mollenkott continued to elaborate by defining absolutization of culture by regarding it as "fundamental" or "only" reality.[33] She then offered examples of the monarchal rule in the Old Testament and slavery in the New Testament as support for her ideas. No one in the modern world would support slavery; therefore, the biblical accounts dealing with this accepted ancient practice are understood to be outdated. Such should be the case for hierarchical human relationships.[34]

She further developed her ideas by commenting on the thoughts of the Apostle Paul. According to Mollenkott, Paul contradicted himself on his position of male/female equality because of his patriarchal socialization.[35] Therefore, one must read his letters more carefully to understand what he meant when he wrote about the roles of men and women in the early church.[36] She cited his letter to the Romans where in chapter 16 Paul mentioned several women: Priscilla, Junia, and Phoebe as fellow Christian workers. However, in 1 Corinthians 11 and 14, Paul wrote restrictions for women in public worship, apparently limiting his position on male/female equality. The cause of this, according to Mollenkott, is his learned socialization.[37]

Therefore, when Mollenkott interpreted passages such as 1 Timothy 2:9–15, she first doubted his authentic authorship, but also questioned his usage of the Genesis creation narratives because they are only poetic, and not didactic in nature. She stressed the importance of understanding the creation narratives as poetry rather than instructional prose. Therefore, Paul's usage of the Genesis passages in his arguments for sex roles in the early church is irrelevant because he used them out of context to prove his patriarchal point of view.[38] Mollenkott concluded that every New Testament passage that deals with male/ female equality does so through a cultural argument, therefore, current understanding of male/female equality must consider what is culturally appropriate as well.[39]

In Galatians 3:28 Paul's statement that "in Christ there is neither male nor female" revolutionized all of the patriarchal order.[40] Literally this statement was Paul breaking out of his old patriarchal ways, and therefore readers today must recognize it for what it is.[41] Mollenkott encouraged her readers that as contemporary interpreters, Scripture must be viewed with all of its contradictions and still allowed "to teach us in what way it was inspired."[42] Paul's human limitations were recorded in Scripture as a model for contemporary usage in struggling with present day issues.[43] Mollenkott urged that Christians today should not and could not "absolutize anything that denies the thrust of the entire Bible toward individual wholeness and harmonious community, toward oneness in the New Creation."[44]

Mollenkott began her hermeneutical statement with this honest approach to the questions she proposed to her new concept of "male-female equality." She wrote:

> The word evidence leads us into consideration of the two problems which most often worry Bible believers when they are confronted with indications that Paul's human limitations show up in his writings and that we cannot continue

absolutizing the biblical culture where women are concerned. The first problem focuses on biblical evidence in general: Can the Bible be used to prove just anything the arguer wants to prove? The second problem is closely related to the first: if we concede that the Bible does teach male-female equality in the home and in the church, then we are admitting that it has been misinterpreted for centuries. Where will the process of reinterpreting the Bible stop, once we make such an admission? Will we be forced into total relativism? Will we lose all sense of absolutes? Will we, by granting male-female equality, in effect be destroying the authority of the Bible over our lives?[45]

From the very beginning, Mollenkott recognized that her ideas called for a different hermeneutical method than was traditionally accepted. In the following pages, she expounded on it.

In answer to the first question Mollenkott proposed in the preceding quote, she answered yes, that the Bible could be used to prove whatever one wished to prove, if only to the acceptability of the person asking. In other words, one could use the Bible to say whatever one wanted it to say, but that did not mean that they used an acceptable approach to arrive at that answer.[46] From here, Mollenkott listed her basic guidelines for reading the Bible.

Her hermeneutical method included consideration for the type of literature being read. Is the passage a "straightforward exposition, intended to explain a concept? Or is it the passage making use of literary forms such as poetry or parable? If the form is literary, what accommodations must be made because of the literary structure?"[47] Mollenkott also regarded word usage in her method, determining first the literal meaning of words and then symbolic meaning in them.[48] Finally, she urged that the context of the passage be understood and appreciated.[49] First, the context of the book of the Bible that one would read from, and then from the context of the entire Word of God.[50]

Mollenkott summarized her remarks on her hermeneutical method in this thought:

> The real way to show respect for the inspiration and authority of the Bible is to trust the Bible to teach us in what way it is inspired. The experience of many serious students of the Bible has taught us that the Bible sometimes records the human limitations of the human beings who were the channels of God's Word to us. How then will we be able to sift out which passages reflect human limitations and which passages reflect the will of God for all times and all places? There is no easy formula. We can do it only by careful study of the text, paying attention to all the methods of precise scholarly interpretation. And we must immediately suspect any reading which contradicts the thrust of the whole Bible toward human justice and oneness in the New Creation.[51]

In the final chapter of *Women, Men, & the Bible* Mollenkott discussed major Bible doctrines relevant to the concepts of male/female equality.

Major Bible Doctrines and Equality

In the concluding chapter of her first book on male/female equality, Mollenkott began by recapturing the need for reconsideration of the traditional roles of men and women. Mollenkott wrote that the early religious feminists thought that the fact that the Bible included examples of women in ministry at all was "amazing and indicative of God's intentions that any women are mentioned at all."[52] She further explained her thoughts, "What biblical feminists see operating in the Bible is the power of God moving in human beings, causing them to overcome the prejudice of their culture in order to include occasional details about women in leadership roles. It is not the small amount of attention to women which is surprising, but rather that there is as much biblical focus on women as actually exists."[53] She went on to state that it was not enough to find evidence in Scripture for the male/female equality position, but that a foundation for these principles must exist in the major Bible doctrines themselves.[54]

The two major Bible doctrines Mollenkott discussed in the conclusion of her book are the incarnation and regeneration.[55] She again reiterated that Jesus became human, *anthropos* in the Greek, rather than male, or *aner*, and pointed to the importance of understanding this fact.[56] She included the discussion on the incarnation because of its significance in understanding the roles of the Trinity and between husband and wife. Traditionalists argue that Jesus submission to the Father "did not imply any inferiority, the Christian woman's subordination in home and church does not imply inferiority to the male- only a different role."[57] But immediately she takes issue with the understanding that the wife's submission to the husband is similar to Christ's submission to the Father.

"To use the analogy that the wife is to the husband as Christ-on-earth is to the Father is to make the male the equivalent of the First Person of the Trinity- and then we are back into the idolatry of the masculine."[58] Mollenkott wrote that the proper understanding of this biblical metaphor is gained in light of the mandate in Ephesians 5 for "the husband to love the wife as Christ loved the church." Wives, therefore, submit only as husbands sacrificially love. This thought is the essence of mutual submission, according to Mollenkott.[59]

She also stressed understanding that when Jesus gave up his will it was not "to some totally external power."[60] Because Jesus and the Father were one, Christ's submission was not to the Father as someone outside of himself. Jesus' "individual will was fused with a universal divine will," therefore, his submission was ultimately to himself. Mollenkott made this point because of her concern that patriarchal socialization ordered women to give up their will to please that of men, therefore crushing the wills of the women under the lives and intentions of men.[61] For Mollenkott, the fact that Jesus essentially submitted to himself redirects the traditional understanding of submission in the context of marriage. In mutual submission, the wife would only submit to what best promotes harmony and the husband would submit by loving his wife towards her personal wholeness and the wholeness of their relationship.[62] Together, they would promote a healthy and respectful mutuality.

IS THE HOMOSEXUAL MY NEIGHBOR?

In 1978, Mollenkott published *Is the Homosexual My Neighbor?* with friend and fellow activist, Letha Dawson Scanzoni. This work formally introduced the issue of homosexuality into the male/female equality debate. The authors divide their thoughts into three sections of the book: understanding the homosexual as neighbor, reasons Christians avoid acceptance of known homosexuals, and the challenge homosexuality presents to American Christendom. Each of these sections is overviewed here.

Understanding the Homosexual as Neighbor

Mollenkott and Scanzoni begin their book with two quotes by Adolf Hitler against homosexuality.[63] They compare the fear and trepidation many Jewish people felt during the Holocaust with the timidity of homosexuals in the modern era. They urge their readers that the issue is complex and must be considered by responsible Christians.[64]

The authors remind their readers of the painful life situations of many homosexual people.[65] They challenge readers that homosexual people outside mainstream patriarchal culture are the ones in "need," similar to that of the story of the neighbor and the Good Samaritan in Luke 10.[66] Mollenkott and Scanzoni reminded their readers that Jesus does not define the neighbor in the account according to race or ethnicity, but according to the one who was in need.[67] They wrote, "Each time we look beyond our neighbor's fears and inadequacies and instead affirm the light that is in every person who ever came into the world (John 1:9), we reinforce our own recognition of the light that is within us."[68]

Reasons Christians Avoid Known Homosexuals

The authors stated that the gay community is "strange territory" for most Christians.[69] The flamboyant behavior of some gay people, the advent of AIDS, and the alternative lifestyle as a whole is different from that experienced by heterosexual Christians.[70] Therefore, to consider accepting homosexuality involves a learning of the challenges and struggles of homosexual people. Ultimately, they maintain that the Bible supports accepting homo-sexual people and their lifestyles, and a comprehensive understanding of the biblical teaching facilitates this acceptance.[71]

The authors began chapter 5 with this thought:

> The Bible does not have a great deal to say about homosexuality, and in the original languages the term itself is never used. Whenever sexual acts between people of the same gender are mentioned in Scripture, the acts are always com-mitted in a very negative context—in the context of, for example, adultery, promiscuity, violence, or idolatrous worship. The fact that this negative context is often ignored may explain why Christians have traditionally shown harsh, unloving, often cruel attitudes toward homosexual people.[72]

They began their biblical case with Genesis 19 and the story of Sodom and Gomorrah.

Genesis 19. Rather than the traditional evangelical interpretation of the condemnation of Sodom and Gomorrah because of their sexually illicit de-mands of the men visiting Abraham, Mollenkott and Scanzoni presented that the real sin involved was that of inhospitality.[73] They acknowledged that the Sodomites' sin is usually understood to be related to homosexuality, "There is no denying that, in the minds of most people, the incident has long been associated with homosexuality. Indeed, the word sodomy is derived from certain interpretations of this biblical passage," yet they expounded on their interpretation in more depth.[74]

"All of this is by way of saying that rather than concentrating on homo-sexuality, the Sodom story seems to be focusing on two specific evils: (1) violent gang rape, and (2) inhospitality to strangers."[75] They expounded on their thought that since the culture was patriarchal, and most of the men of Sodom and Gomorrah were likely heterosexual, so their crime was more heinous because they were "seeking to humiliate the strangers."[76] Ultimately the problem at issue with the Sodom story is their demand for violence and unwillingness to treat the visitors with kindness, while never specifically mentioning the issue of homosexuality at all.[77]

Leviticus 18:22, 20:13. Next, the authors moved to the Levitical prohibitions concerning sexual morality in Leviticus 18:22 and 20:13. The authors under-stood these passages to be addressing fertility worship practices of the surround-ing pagan nations.[78] They point out that the key concept to keep in mind was that in condemning acts of sexuality during worship, the "warnings and condemna-tions in these various passages are centered around the idolatrous practices of the fertility religions, not whether the ceremonial sexual activity involved men with men or men with women. The people who loved and served the God of Israel were strictly forbidden to have anything to do with idolatry."[79]

Romans 1:26–27 and Matthew 19. The Apostle Paul, in the letter to the Romans, presented the acts of homosexuality as "unnatural," therefore making it the next text that Mollenkott and Scanzoni addressed. Furthering their argument that the Bible does not prohibit homosexuality in general, but acts done outside a loving, committed relationship the authors continued their interpretation of each Scripture addressing homosexuality. They wrote:

> The key thoughts seem to be lust, "unnaturalness," and, in verse 28, a desire to avoid acknowledgement of God. But although the censure fits the idolatrous people with whom Paul was concerned here, it does not fit the case of a sincere homosexual Christian. Such a person loves Jesus Christ and wants above all to acknowledge God in all of life, yet for some unknown reason feels drawn to someone of the same sex- not because of lust, but because of sincere, heartfelt love.[80]

The authors furthered their interpretation of Romans 1 by stating that Paul's argument for understanding what is "natural" has cultural implications.[81] Expressions of what natural or unnatural sexuality change from one society to the next, therefore, Mollenkott and Scanzoni stated that Paul's condemnation in Romans 1:26–27 has no lasting significance for committed homosexual relationships[82]

The bottom line for the authors on "what the Bible says" about homosexuality is that it never specifically even mentions it. They stated that the actual word never even appears in the original languages to begin with, in addition to the fact that the concept of a loving relationship is never discussed either.[83] The authors went to detailed lengths to discuss Scriptures that are traditionally understood as prohibiting this form of sexuality with arguments in favor of homosexuality based on contextual evidence of traditional interpretations and cultural relevancy for the practice in the twenty-first century.

The Challenge to American Christendom

Concluding with their call for American Christianity to accept and support the plight of the homosexual, the authors confronted issues preventing adequate aid for homosexuals. They wrote:

> If the church takes seriously its responsibility to share Christ's love with all people, Christians must reach out to homosexual people as well as heterosexual people. That will mean not only giving serious attention to the findings of the social and behavioral sciences, but also facing up to a number of specific issues relating to the topic of homosexuality. First, we must deal with homophobia. . . . Second, we need to develop an understanding of gay people as a people or

community. And third, we must ask ourselves if there needs to be a rethinking of homosexuality from a biblical and theological perspective.[84]

Caring for people who are both homosexual and heterosexual is costly. However, Mollenkott and Scanzoni reminded their readers of the fact that Jesus honored the Good Samaritan who counted the cost and took care of his neighbor. In raising the question of "Is the homosexual my neighbor?" the authors presented American Christianity in the late 1970s with a question that continues to shadow the church in the early twenty-first century.

In the 1994 revised and updated edition, the authors summarized their intentions:

> Our hope in writing this book is that many of our readers will be willing to examine the evidence and correct any misconceptions they may have held about gay, lesbian, and bisexual people, learning to love all their neighbors as themselves. At the same time, we know that some readers may be emotionally resistant to new evidence and new ways of looking at their homosexual neighbor.[85]

Citing many of the "continuing challenges" of the church and society in general since its first printing, Mollenkott and Scanzoni persisted in their call for a new homosexual ethic. They referred to many current happenings and developments that have prevented further acceptance of the homosexual ethic in the revised edition of 1994. Their fundamental argument centered on the fact that homosexual people experience much pain and prejudice in society and the church, therefore, Christians much begin to see them as their "neighbor" and act accordingly.

THE DIVINE FEMININE: THE BIBLICAL IMAGERY OF GOD AS FEMALE

In 1983 Mollenkott elaborated on her thoughts for re-imaging God in her next book, *The Divine Feminine: Biblical Imagery of God as Female*. To advance her movement into feminism meant to articulate clearly the female imaging of God. Therefore, Mollenkott contributed to the task in this book that considered certain feminine images of God in the Bible that were not traditionally noticed or mentioned. She wrote, "With relatively little effort, grammar can be manipulated so that females as well as males are included and affirmed."[86]

Mollenkott furthered the concept of mutual submission by re-imaging God.[87] As men and women understand God as both male and female, this understanding would contribute to a shared humanity. If God is male and female, then human existence could be shared easier rather than regarded as patriarchal rule. She wrote that a "mutuality in the Godhead contributes to a mutuality in understanding gender."[88]

Feminine God Images throughout History

Mollenkott reasoned, "If, indeed, images of God as female are present in the text of the Bible, it would be logical to assume that people would have noticed them long before the 1980s."[89] She cited the thought of Clement of Alexandria as being one of the first persons to speak of "Mother God."[90] Mollenkott also included the feminine language for God found in the apocryphal book *Acts of Peter,* which especially supported mutual submission.[91] She also lists many other church history figures such as John Chrysostom and Saint Ambrose.[92]

Mollenkott was convinced that feminine God imagery was supported through biblical and theological history. She wrote, "Feminine God language is a step in the direction of enrichment."[93] Not only did it support the liberation of oppressed females, it also contributed to a clearer mutuality in human existence. This human existence included struggle for social justice. Mollenkott wrote that the more feminine God language was accepted into Christianity, the more the concerns of social justice would be stressed.

GODDING: HUMAN RESPONSIBILITY AND THE BIBLE

Mollenkott continued to expand her understanding of the biblical mandate to "love your neighbor" in her next book, *Godding: Human Responsibility and the Bible.* Her thesis was, "Human responsibility, in its deepest and fullest dimension, entails godding, an embodiment or incarnation of God's love in human flesh, with the goal of co creating with God a just and loving human society."[94] She elaborated:

> I think 1 John 4:16–17 is a passage about godding: God is love, and [the one who] abides in love abides in God, and God abides in [that one]. In this is love perfected with us, that we may have confidence for the Day of Judgment, because as [God] is, so are we in this world. (RSV, emphasis and inclusive language mine).[95]

Therefore, Mollenkott redefined "loving one's neighbor" as godding, elaborating on the specifics of that responsibility in the development of her thesis.

Godding, according to Mollenkott, is the opposite way of relating to people through patriarchal rule.[96] When a Christian relates to another person by godding, then they are loving and supportive rather than lording over them their authority. In this way, a man or woman leads effectively, according to Mollenkott. The godding approach to leadership is in direct opposition to patriarchal rule, and it should be. The reason a person leads differently in the godding approach is because they respect the sacred presence of God in all human beings.[97] Godding through leadership involved recognizing the God within myself and others, and therefore respecting the God in them. Mollenkott explained it:

> To recognize that God is becoming God's Self through the process of my living is emphatically not the same as worshiping myself. To worship myself would be to make the very stupid mistake of assuming that one aspect of an enormously complex being or process is the entire being or process. I really am one embodiment or manifestation or incarnation of God, but I am not God. I am part of that "all" that God is "above," and "in," and "through." but my infinitesimal parameters do not contain the whole of who God is.[98]

The process of godding attempted to overcome the patriarchal way of leading through authority structure, and employ newer doctrines of God at the same time.

Godding toward Religious Inclusiveness

In a section called "A Theology of the Wind," Mollenkott wrote:

> Because I am a Christian and because I think my own family of faith needs to learn inclusiveness perhaps more than any other, I must now utilize specifically Christian terminology. It is my conviction that godding, a conscious cooperation infused with the Holy Spirit, calls us toward an all-inclusive attitude, a theology of the wind, a relationship to God and the world that does not try to make things easy by ruling out whole areas of human experience and whole groups of human beings.[99]

Thus, her inclusivism was goal oriented. Mollenkott believed that through godding and religious inclusivism, patriarchy would be tranformed. Patriarchal rule was the enemy of all women and marginalized people in general; therefore the way of godding was the liberation of the oppressed through mutual submission and service. Inherent in its practice, however, was an attitude of acceptance and hospitality to people of all faiths and religions, thus her inclusivism developed.

Mollenkott's ideas on the use of language followed suit in her argument for religious inclusivism. In fact, the movement to become more religiously inclusive was dependent on the use of inclusive language.[100] She argued that because the human mind is literal, the language one used must be literal as well.[101] Therefore, God must be referred to as He or She and language of the Bible must be altered to reflect this fact. Mollenkott concluded this chapter by admonishing her readers that they would need courage to address these issues in contemporary evangelical culture and belief.

Mollenkott commented on guidance for the practice of godding by returning to her earlier theme of balance. She wrote:

> But Christian humanists are suggesting, and I agree, that instead of forgetting the Bible we confront it in a contextual and holistic way. Although it inevitably reflects many of the harsh realities of the sexist, racist, and classist cultures in which the biblical authors lived, it is also alive with insight and significance. The roots of our Judeo-Christian tradition are biblical roots. While it is imperative that we grow into a more truly inclusive society, we will not grow by hacking away our roots.[102]

For Mollenkott, growing to be more inclusive and accepting the roots of Christianity were a part of godding, of accepting the human responsibility to create a just and loving society. Implications of this practice reached every aspect of society, therefore, furthering the movement away from patriarchal oppression into the New Creation.

SENSUOUS SPIRITUALITY: OUT FROM FUNDAMENTALISM

The 1993 publication of Mollenkott further developed her ideas of the applications necessary for re-imaging God as feminine and "godding" begun in her earlier works. In the introduction of this book Mollenkott wrote:

> I believe that there is One Ultimate Interrelational Being who under girds all personhood and relationships, One Consciousness that flows through all consciousness, One Love that is unconditional and embraces everything that lives (and everything does live). My name for this Cosmic Energy or Consciousness is God. I dislike the word Goddess because in our social context that word implies the presence of a second All-Encompassing Being—surely a contradiction in terms and logic. In a human race constituted of half males and half females, the term God ought to imply the presence of a Goddess-component just as strongly as the term Goddess implies the presence of a God component: but after centuries of heteropatriarchal emphasis on male separateness, autonomy, and individualism, it doesn't.[103]

In this work, Mollenkott defined more specifically the area of her ministry focus. More and more she felt called to be a voice for the lesbian, bisexual, gay, transgender community within evangelicalism. At this point in her ministry, Mollenkott identified patriarchalism, and specifically heteropatriarchalism, or patriarchy perpetuated by compulsory heterosexuality, as prime opponents of mutual service and partnership. Therefore, Mollenkott marked this territory as her primary ministry goal: to revolutionize the legacy of patriarchal oppression in society.[104]

The Heart of the Matter

Personal journey motivated Mollenkott's movement into this area. She wrote:

> So how does a fundamentalist who believes she is essentially and totally depraved become transformed into a person who knows she is an innocent spiritual being who is temporarily having human experiences? The answer is: through a long and gradual process involving the study of hermeneutics; a great deal of dreaming and learning to interpret those dreams; extensive journaling; psychological use of the I Ching and the Tarot to learn something about the movement of my unconscious mind; agonizing struggles with A Course in Miracles; studying the words of Paul Normal Tuttle; reading up on the hermetic tradition and on spiritual healing; much pondering of great theological poets like John Milton and Emily Dickinson; listening to and reading outstanding thinkers among my contemporaries; learning how to love and be loved; the experience of my mother's death and thereafter our continued closeness; here and there, some psychotherapy; and some mildly mystical experiences.[105]

The validity of personal experience only increased in the expansion of Mollenkott's thought. She believed:

> After all, everyone else at their core is exactly who I am: undivided from God Herself, ultimately secure in a love that can never be broken. Whether or not we are able to recognize each other's holiness during this little life, I believe that eventually we all will rejoice together in the bliss of universal at-one-ment.[106]

Since each person's experience is trustworthy and informative, then their spirituality must also be acceptable and understood. Mollenkott wrote that the thesis of this book was:

> That spiritual beings who are having human experiences—at least those with activist temperaments—demonstrate love for their ultimate and eternal context by enacting tender concern for the penultimate and the apparently temporary. In other words, sensuous spirituality breeds concern for the well being of the

people and all the other creatures who are here on this planet at this time, and for the planet itself. By seeking direction from the Inner Guide at the center of her Self, a human being can glimpse the larger picture in which no person, group, or nation is more important than any other person, group, or nation.[107]

Mollenkott began support for her thesis by comparing the story of two handmaids. The first was a character taken from Margaret Atwood's novel *The Handmaid's Tale* who is a handmaid against her own will. She is not pleased to be in this role, and rebels in it. The second handmaid Mollenkott considered was the Virgin Mary. This handmaid accepted her position as the "Lord's handmaid" and came to prominence because of it. Mollenkott argued that both examples of the handmaids are necessary today to build a better understanding of mutuality in partnership.

The Bible in Support of Human Diversity

She also elaborated on her move from traditional hermeneutics to interpretive communities in accepting and affirming all humanity. Mollenkott wrote:

> Here I want to explain why I myself switched from the traditional hermeneutics I believed for the first thirty-five years of my life to the pluralistic hermeneutics I have outlined here. In the first place, as a woman (and a lesbian woman at that) I was desperate. Like the Greek woman who became creative and assertive because she was desperate for the healing of her daughter, I was desperate for authenticity, for the healing of my self esteem, and for the use of my gifts.[108]

The goal for Mollenkott was to be fully alive; therefore, whatever was necessary facilitated this liveliness was acceptable in her biblical interpretation. This value motivated her support for the lesbian, bisexual, gay, transsexual community because they represented the most diversity within society.

Eros as Spiritual Urge

Mollenkott moved next to the development of a spiritual understanding of sexuality. Quoting the philosopher Schopenhauer, she built on the idea that "sexual passion is the kernel of the will to live."[109] She identified *eros* as more than an expression of lust or sexual longing. This term came to mean sex, friendship, co-creational activity, and common concern for the welfare of another.[110] In this sense, Mollenkott broadened the traditional understanding of the Greek term *eros* to support her ideas.

Mollenkott also wrote, "I have no objection to the casual sharing of sexual pleasure and tenderness except to note that people who never get beyond recreational sex eventually report boredom with it."[111] She reinterpreted the story of Naomi and Ruth as same sex lovers, to support the possibility of this idea; however not one passage was indicated to support her view clearly from Scripture. Ultimately, Mollenkott used the Genesis 2:18 principle that "it is not good for man to be alone" to strengthen her argument that *eros* is spiritual urge. She reasoned that if it is not good for man (or woman according to her) to be alone, then however one is oriented to express one's sexual spirituality is acceptable as long as it is respectful and does no harm to another human being.[112]

More Functional Families

She concluded her development of the thesis of *Sensuous Spirituality* with a discussion of interpretive communities. Mollenkott identified this particular awareness as basic to all hermeneutical methods.[113] She wrote, "So the one really foolish assumption is that anyone could possibly arrive at a situationless, culture-free, objective interpretation of any text, let alone a text as complex as the Bible."[114] Her belief in objectivity had been abandoned because the search for meaning is always situated within individual and community shared experience.

Mollenkott argued passionately for the necessity of social change based on this belief that truth is interpreted by an individual through agreement with the interpretive community in which one finds oneself. In her understanding, therefore, social justice comes as individuals within their interpretive communities are willing to become active, thus connecting her concern for social activism on the behalf of the lesbian, bisexual, gay, transsexual community. She wrote, "If activism is part of our nature and we feel stimulus toward justice work when we are centered, then God wants to express Her loving justice through our activism."[115] In other words, as the spiritually sensuous, "demonstrate their love for their ultimate and eternal context by enacting tender concern" for those inside and outside their communities, society is changed and improved. Mollenkott identified this as "heaven on earth."[116] It was her understanding of the way to achieve the New Creation.

OMNIGENDER

Virginia Ramey Mollenkott continued her theological development as evidenced in the publication of *Omnigender*.[117] She discussed her concerns with the gender crisis in Western culture through three major sections of her book. For the purposes of this overview, these sections are called the gender crisis: injustices and inequities; the gender crisis: Judaism, Christianity, and other religions; the gender crisis: the new society.

Mollenkott wrote, "This book is my attempt to move beyond the binary gender construct in order to set forth a new gender paradigm, which seeks to include and offer liberation to everyone who has been oppressed by the old model."[118] She was working from the liberation theology model of oppression and freedom; however, in this work she applied these concepts further to her concept of heteropatriarchy. Mollenkott redefined this term to be the freedom of oppression from compulsory heterosexualism, rather than simply freedom from the oppression of traditional men's and women's roles.

Her interpretation of Galatians 3:28 also progressed further in this book. In earlier works, Mollenkott wrote that Galatians 3:28 was a central theme for biblical equality, as defined as the obliteration of sex roles in Christ. However, in this work, she reverted back to a literal translation of the verse. In other words, her thought altered to accepting that Paul in this verse might have literally meant that in Christ no male or female binary dichotomy exists. Christ gave individuals the opportunity to be authentic about which gender or combination of maleness or femaleness they sensed they had been created to be.[119]

The Gender Crisis: Injustices and Inequities

The alternative to a binary gender construct was omnigender, or to allow individuals to embody their own gender or combination of genders honestly and openly.[120] Since sexuality is basically a social construct that changes from culture to culture, the answer is to change the injustice's within culture. Therefore, Mollenkott devoted the rest of the book to outlining why Western culture needs this change and how it can be ushered in socially, politically and religiously. Beginning to give her ideas a spiritual basis, she wrote:

> I agree with Chicana Gloria Anzaldua, who argues that when people are 'queer'—gay, lesbian, bisexual, transgender, or off-norm in any other fashion—it is because real gods, goddesses, and/or spirits have chosen those people to embody or incarnate them. Although I believe in only one Divine Source, not a multitude of gods and goddesses, I have certainly noticed that that One Source likes variety and has chosen to be incarnated in millions of diverse ways.[121]

Therefore, constructing a society that accepts and values alternative expressions of sexuality and gender must be constructed to alleviate the suffering imposed by traditional gender constructs.

The Gender Crisis: Judaism, Christianity, and Other Religions

Mollenkott began building her basis for an omnigender society based on religious principles. She reiterated earlier thought that Christians can no longer base their sexual ethics on biological testing because of its insufficiencies.[122] Therefore, she moved to another interpretation of the Genesis creation accounts. In this portion of her argument from Christianity, Mollenkott noted that humanity was hermaphroditic at first inception. From Genesis 1:27 when the text says that God created them "male and female," Mollenkott reasoned that the first creation of Adam constituted elements of both maleness and femaleness, not one or the other, but a combination of both.[123]

Interestingly, Mollenkott progressed from this discussion into her thoughts on salvation. She wrote:

> What then is the salvation that is embodied in our Savior Jesus Christ? For those who believe in Original Blessing, it is that we and our divine Source are and always have been one, that the imagined separation never occurred, that God's sovereign will could not be overturned, and that God's love for us is endless, irrevocable, and unconditional. From a religious perspective, Jesus was crucified because he insisted that he and his divine Source were one, which sounded like blasphemy to the religious leaders of his place and time.[124]

For Mollenkott, a discussion of the original creation of man was linked to the definition of salvation because men and women incarnated God from the very beginning. This connection with the hermaphroditic interpretation of Genesis 1 only strengthened her argument for an omnigender society.

From this reinterpretation of Genesis 1, Mollenkott further developed her ideas on hermeneutical method. In this portion of her ideological progression Mollenkott reiterated her newfound discovery that Adam and Eve were early transgender archetypes. She connected her ideas with an ancient Hebrew understanding of the text as well. She wrote:

> For our purposes here, the important point is that both Jewish and Christian scholarship has recognized that the original created being is either hermaphroditic or sexually undifferentiated, a 'gender outlaw' by modern terms, closer to a transgender identity than to half of a binary gender construct.[125]

Basically, Mollenkott paralleled Old Testament prohibitions of temple prostitution from Deuteronomy 23:17 with avoidance of Canaanite polytheistic religion.[126] Cross dressing, homosexuality, and temple prostitution were all closely connected in this religion; therefore, Mollenkott connected the prohibition for this activity with the instruction for the Israelites to be strictly monotheistic. However, in modern culture when polytheism is much less practiced, Mollenkott argued that prohibitions against cross-dressing and homosexuality no longer apply. She returned to her argument that homosexuality in the context of a loving relationship was never forbidden in the Bible.[127]

The New Testament theological concept of the Virgin Birth is in itself, according to Mollenkott, an intersexual theme.[128] How else would a young

woman who never had sex with a man become pregnant? Mollenkott maintained that the birth was parthenogenetic, that the Virgin from a biological
perspective contained both male and female features. Another transgender
example is found in the story of the Roman centurion in Matthew 8:5–13. In
this story, Jesus honored the centurion's request for healing for his servant.
However, Mollenkott argued that since the centurion referred to his servant as
"his boy," he was probably also his lover because in Greek culture at that time
this term could have been used to refer to a younger lover/ friend.[129] Mollenkott concluded her New Testament support for transgender acceptance with
the example of the Body of Christ as a whole. Since the Body contains both
men and women, and the image is primarily feminine in nature and Christ is
both male and female, the entire image of the Body is intersexual.[130]

The Gender Crisis: The New Society

She proposed that everyone would be able to enact the gender they felt themselves to be. However, not only would each individual enact either male or
female, but also his or her own combination of the two. Mollenkott's descrip-
tion of herself as a "masculine woman" comes into focus here. She thought
that babies born intersexual should be considered unisexual until they had
the opportunity to indicate what sex they felt themselves to be.[131] Eventually
therefore, no legal or governmental documents would include a person's sex
for identification purposes. Also bathrooms would all be unisexual, without
differentiation.[132] Basically, the ultimate goal of an omnigender society would
be an acceptance of the full range of sexual and gender identities, from the
most feminine of females to the most masculine of males and all gradations
in between.

Ultimately, Mollenkott rested her case for omnigender society on her
evolved interpretation of Galatians 3:28. If the Apostle Paul is to be taken
literally, and Mollenkott concluded in *Omnigender* that he could be, then
no prestige difference should exist between males and females in the New
Creation.[133] "As beloved siblings stemming from one Divine Spirit" an
omnigender society is an ideal for people working toward a just and loving
society today.

CONCLUSION

The purpose of this chapter was to overview Virginia Ramey Mollenkott's
major theological and academic contributions. Mollenkott's devotion to
feminist philosophy, by her own admission, seriously altered her life and

beliefs. At the time when she was wrestling with difficult decisions in her marriage and divorce, feminism offered an alternative to her fundamentalist understanding of Scripture. As she embraced this ideology, her beliefs about God and his word also changed. Chapter 4 will address the major themes apparent in her theology, while chapter 5 will analyze Mollenkott's theological growth.

NOTES

1. Virginia R. Mollenkott, *Adamant & Stone Chips: A Christian Humanist Approach to Knowledge* (Waco, TX: Word, 1968), 11.
2. Ibid., 21.
3. Ibid., 22.
4. Ibid.
5. Ibid., 41.
6. Virginia R. Mollenkott, *In Search of Balance* (Waco, TX: Word, 1969), 13.
7. Ibid., 14.
8. Ibid., 15.
9. Ibid., 22.
10. Ibid., 138–89.
11. Ibid., 150.
12. Virginia R. Mollenkott, *Women, Men, & the Bible* (Nashville: Abingdon, 1977), ix.
13. Ibid., 1.
14. Ibid., 2.
15. Ibid., 2–4.
16. Ibid., 8.
17. Ibid., 11.
18. Ibid., 29–31.
19. Ibid., 36.
20. Ibid., 39.
21. Ibid., 40.
22. Ibid., 46.
23. Ibid.
24. Ibid., 47.
25. Ibid.
26. Ibid., 52.
27. Ibid., 53.
28. Ibid., 61.
29. Ibid., 62–63.
30. Ibid., 62.
31. Ibid., 74.
32. Ibid., 74.

33. Ibid.
34. Ibid., 77.
35. Ibid.
36. Ibid., 78.
37. Ibid., 82.
38. Ibid., 84.
39. Ibid.
40. Ibid.
41. Ibid.
42. Ibid., 86.
43. Ibid.
44. Ibid., 87.
45. Ibid., 88.
46. Ibid., 89.
47. Ibid., 91.
48. Ibid., 92–93.
49. Ibid., 92.
50. Ibid., 93.
51. Ibid., 98.
52. Ibid., 100.
53. Ibid.
54. Ibid., 101.
55. Ibid.
56. Ibid.
57. Ibid., 102.
58. Ibid., 103.
59. Ibid., 104.
60. Ibid., 105.
61. Ibid.
62. Ibid., 106.
63. Letha Scanzoni and Virginia R. Mollenkott, *Is the Homosexual My Neighbor? Another Christian View* (San Francisco: Harper and Row, 1978) 1.
64. Ibid., 4.
65. Ibid., 9.
66. Ibid., 10.
67. Ibid.
68. Ibid., 9.
69. Ibid., 46.
70. Ibid.
71. Ibid., 55.
72. Ibid., 56.
73. Ibid., 57
74. Ibid.
75. Ibid., 59.
76. Ibid., 58.

77. Ibid., 60.

78. Ibid., 63.

79. Ibid., 63.

80. Ibid., 67.

81. Ibid., 68.

82. Ibid.

83. Ibid., 56.

84. Ibid., 103.

85. Ibid., 158.

86. Virginia R. Mollenkott, *The Divine Feminine: Imaging God as Female* (New York: Crossroad, 1983), 1.

87. Ibid., 2.

88. Ibid.

89. Ibid., 8.

90. Ibid.

91. Ibid.

92. Ibid.

93. Ibid., 13.

94. Virginia R. Mollenkott, *Godding: Human Responsibility and the Bible* (New York: Crossroad, 1987), 2.

95. Ibid.

96. Ibid.

97. Ibid.

98. Ibid.

99. Ibid., 39.

100. Ibid., 51.

101. Ibid.

102. Ibid.

103. Mollenkott, *Sensuous Spirituality*, 10–11.

104. Ibid., 13.

105. Ibid., 16.

106. Ibid., 17.

107. Ibid., 21.

108. Ibid., 68–69.

109. Ibid., 96.

110. Ibid., 99.

111. Ibid.

112. Ibid., 113.

113. Ibid., 186.

114. Ibid., 167–68.

115. Ibid., 186.

116. Ibid., 187.

117. Virginia R. Mollenkott, *Omnigender* (Cleveland: Pilgrim, 2001), v.

118. Ibid., vii.

119. Ibid., viii.

120. Ibid., 8.
121. Ibid., 16.
122. Ibid., 85.
123. Ibid.
124. Ibid., 87.
125. Ibid., 91.
126. Ibid., 98.
127. Ibid., 100.
128. Ibid., 105.
129. Ibid., 108.
130. Ibid., 110.
131. Ibid., 167.
132. Ibid., 168.
133. Ibid., 192.

Chapter Four

An Analysis of the Religious Feminist Theology of Virginia Ramey Mollenkott

This chapter analyzes the major theological themes evident in a comprehensive understanding of the religious feminist approach of Virginia Ramey Mollenkott. These themes are drawn from her publications from her first book, *Adamant and Stone Chips* in 1967 to her final book, *Transgender Journeys*, published in 2003. Her ideas are ordered according to her chronological and conceptual development.

CHRISTIAN HUMANISM

Early on Mollenkott stated her support of a Christian humanist approach to life, education, and theology. She wrote:

> The term *Christian humanism* is the attempt to encompass in two words the two aspects of each of us which must be given their due if we are to live abundantly. We are *Christian*, but we are also *human*. Following Christ's pattern, we need to increase in favor with God and man. According to First John, there is no point in deceiving ourselves that we love God if we do not manifest loving interest in our fellow human beings. The Christian humanist attempts to hold in fruitful interaction both Christ and human culture, subordinating the human to Christ, attempting to bring every thought into captivity to the obedience of Christ, yet not denying the dignity and value and responsibility of being human.[1]

Several factors contributed to her support of this philosophy. The approach of Christian humanism takes seriously the acquisition and pursuit of knowledge. It is an approach that particularly admires excellence in the artistic and literary world.[2] Human relationships also serve as a hub for determining appropriate and acceptable ideas. As she grew personally in her academic abilities, this view that prioritizes excellence in human endeavors of all kinds became increasingly important.

The Influence of Intellectualism

Based on Mollenkott's own admission, the theme of Christian humanism can be identified as one of her most important theological emphases. However, several factors contributed to her acceptance of this approach. Her keen intellect motivated Mollenkott's need for thoughtful Christian faith. This section considers three main contributing factors that the influence of intellect had on her acceptance of Christian humanism.

Mollenkott's Fundamentalist Background

From her earliest writing, Mollenkott was open about her experiences from her Plymouth Brethren upbringing. As a young girl, Mollenkott took the teaching of her religious authorities seriously. The messages that she heard from her church, especially about the wicked nature of the human heart, seemed to have significant resonance with Mollenkott, partly because of incest and beatings during her early childhood. She recounted her early attempts to memorize Scripture to counter these messages.[3] For Mollenkott, who experienced more family tragedy at the age of nine (her dad's departure from her home), the messages of the church were contradictory with her experiences with them during personal tragedy.

When she was beaten while walking home from her predominantly black school at the age of nine, Mollenkott recounted no offer of help or comfort from her religious authorities. When she experienced shame from a sexual relationship with an older member of her church, her mother and the religious leaders in her life only contributed to her pain and struggle by sending her away without her consent to a boarding school.[4] In later years, she also wrote about her secret struggles with lesbianism during her early life. Each of these experiences contributed to Mollenkott's growing sense that something about her early religious life was insufficient. The fundamentalist beliefs of her parents and grandparents were painful and restrictive to Mollenkott. The restrictive, unfulfilling approaches of extreme fundamentalism only confounded her personal and theological development.

Mollenkott's Educational Experiences

As Mollenkott tried to reconcile her painful personal experiences through the lens of fundamentalism, her intellect catapulted her up the academic ladder. Although she chose to attend Bob Jones University, a religiously fundamental school, her intellectual passions grew. She wrote of being taught various religious precepts that did not seem to coincide with her growing body of knowledge. For instance, Mollenkott mentioned this experience:

> When I was in high school and college, people used to assure me that I was trying too hard to be a good Christian. All I really had to do was "let go and let God." And I wanted to do exactly that. But let go of what? And let God do what? And how to let go? And how to let God? Nobody was very handy with the answers to those questions. In fact, I hardly dared frame the questions in my mind. They seemed impious and disrespectful. Anybody really spiritual wouldn't need to inquire.[5]

As this quote illustrates, Mollenkott took her spirituality seriously though she struggled often to make sense of it in light of her experiences.

Throughout graduate work on her Master's and doctoral degrees, Mollenkott taught in university settings. While she sought to apply her thoughts in the classroom, her educational experiences continued to broaden her thinking and understanding of life. In her books, she often criticized people of faith who questioned the pursuit of knowledge and excellence therein. She wrote:

> Anyone who has taught at the high school or college level can testify, as I can, that anti-intellectualism and/or anti-humanism is a strong strain in the United States, particularly in Protestantism. And the more conservative the political and religious stance, the more anti-intellectual other attitudes tend to become (although of course there are some brilliant exceptions).[6]

Her personal educational experiences alongside her professional teaching experiences convinced Mollenkott of the need for Christian humanism, or a view in which both the human experience and divine endeavor are appreciated together.

Mollenkott's dissertation: Milton and the Apocrypha

If "Christian humanism subordinates the human to the divine because of the creature's proper relationship to the Creator," then Mollenkott's most influential encounter with this sort of thinking came from her doctoral dissertation research on John Milton.[7] As a literary author who dealt with theological issues, Mollenkott encountered in Milton a meeting of both her passions for literature and theology. During this time, Mollenkott admits that it was Milton's treatment of sexuality and divorce that began to cause her to question her beliefs on these and many other topics.[8] Mollenkott recounted the time that she, "stood in the New York Public Library, amazed and awed by an entire wall of card catalogue drawers devoted to works of biblical scholarship."[9] Her research brought her face to face with a Christian who dealt with topics in a way that was both intellectual and thoughtful, and for Mollenkott this approach epitomized Christian humanism.

Mollenkott also attributed her introduction to the new hermeneutical practices to Milton.[10] While she was studying and teaching during her doctoral research, her marriage continued to become less than satisfying. As she encountered Milton's interpretation of the Bible, she applied his hermeneutics to areas that were relevant to her life. Thus, upon completing her doctoral work on Milton, she divorced her husband. Therefore, again her intellectual and academic development contributed to her movement into Christian humanism. Milton, according to Mollenkott, advocated a hermeneutic that was more nuanced and precise than the selectively literal reading of her Plymouth Brethren background.[11] Therefore, her time reading and studying his ideas influenced her growing admiration for Christian humanism.

Appreciation for the Arts and Culture

Central to the concepts of Christian humanism is narrowing "the gap between Christianity and human cultural achievement."[12] Therefore, a growing appreciation for the arts as an expression of human endeavor is a natural part of this philosophy.[13] Her natural inclination for literature made it easier for Mollenkott to accept this part of Christian humanism. Two aspects of artistic and cultural appreciation that contributed to her emphasis on Christian humanism are considered here.

The Role of English Literature

As Mollenkott encountered literature during her academic journey, she was introduced to a much broader worldview than that of the fundamentalism of her young life. Her encounter with literature affected the way that Mollenkott viewed faith and learning. Educational theory according to Christian humanism is a holistic approach that includes an appreciation for the fine arts.[14] As the artist expresses his own image of God through his creativity, the reader or observer communes with the artist and ultimately with God through the art. Therefore, as Mollenkott encountered literature in her journey through the lens of Christian humanism her understanding of life broadened.

As Mollenkott encountered works of literature through her education, she had the choice of filtering her knowledge through a strict epistemology given to her by her Plymouth Brethren background, or through the lens of Christian humanists who appreciated all human expressions of art and life. Her second book, *In Search of Balance*, is devoted to arguing for this new, balanced approach she had discovered.[15] She wrote:

> I have lost my balance—that is, if I ever really had any. I guess the fact is that I never really had any. It was not very many years ago that this awful realization hit me. I had lived without balance because I had not really known who I was. Actually, I had not even known what I liked or didn't like. Don't misunderstand me. I had achieved a Ph.D., and on the surface I looked anything but indecisive. My lack of balance stemmed from a tacitly assumed concept of God which had turned me into a drifter.[16]

Therefore, her developing loyalty to Christian humanism strengthened through her love and appreciation for the arts.

The Call for Unified Vision

Increasingly, Mollenkott was convinced that the way to approach all of life was contradictory to the way that she had been taught as a young child.

> Christian humanism seeks to affirm a unified vision, a liberating realization that in spite of the fall of man, Christ Jesus remains the King and God remains all-powerful—the motivating force in human history. This is not to deny that man has perverted and debauched what he was intended to be and do by his sinful choice of self rather than God; but it is to assert the reality of Christ's redemptive work and the ultimate sovereignty of God the creator.[17]

In her fundamentalist upbringing where she was taught that the heart of man is wicked and never to be trusted, she found her intellect and personhood invalidated.[18] However, in Christian humanism she became convinced of the need both for an appreciation for God and for human endeavor. The term that brought these two ideas together in Christian humanism is the "unified vision." This vision is a commitment both to a relationship with God through Jesus, and a relationship with mankind through an appreciation for the arts and intellectual pursuit.

This dedication to the unified vision continued to influence Mollenkott throughout the development of her theology. In its early stages, she embraced the teaching according to an appreciation for human life and its expressions of art and literature. However, as Mollenkott encountered various forms of religion her commitment to the unified vision was expanded.[19] What began early on in her thought as a simple approval of God and humanity grew to the acceptance and affirmation of the fallen nature of and effects of sin. However, adherence to and the influence of the theme of the Christian humanist unified vision exists throughout the development of Mollenkott's theology.

Love as the Guiding Principle

"Christian humanism seeks to affirm the importance of human relationships as a proof (not a cause, but an inevitable result) of genuine salvation."[20] Therefore, to love your neighbor as yourself is an overarching theme in all of Christian humanism. For Mollenkott, it is central in her understanding of relationships because of her commitment to highly valuing all of life and human endeavor particularly.

She wrote, "The passage of Scripture which is perhaps most pertinent to the Christian humanist world-view is the thirteenth chapter of First Corinthians."[21] She cited the text of 1 Corinthians 13 as presenting a "hierarchy of values" wherein love outranks knowledge and the pursuit of knowledge.[22] She believed that "ideas and causes are temporal, but people are eternal. To mistreat a human being because his ideas differ from mine is thus to harm an eternal being because of a temporal, ephemeral matter."[23] Ultimately because people are made in the image of God their personhood is to be valued over their ideas; hence, relationships with people are to be valued over the search for knowledge and its communication. Therefore, when assigning importance and priority in one's worldview, love must be the determining factor in accepting or rejecting a belief system.

In Mollenkott's Christian humanist paradigm, love is the guiding principle for matters of life and faith because human life and personhood are valued more highly than knowledge itself. Early on she attested to the unreliable nature of knowledge in general depending on the interpretation.[24] Therefore, the bottom line for Mollenkott was love. Mollenkott's commitment to love being her guiding principle in relationships and pursuit of knowledge first developed in her Christian humanist approach.

FEMINISM

The second major theme evident in the theology of Virginia Ramey Mollenkott is her commitment to feminism. Her encounters with feminism were first published in 1977 in *Women, Men, & the Bible*. They had specific effects on her life, in particular her marriage. This section considers the progression of her thought through her adherence to the basic tenets of feminist ideology.

The Meaning of Equality

Mollenkott believed that the "Christian way of relating" was that of mutual submission or mutuality with respect to male/female relationships.[25] A man would relate to a woman out of mutuality based on the concept that they were equal in worth and in status. No distinguishing characteristics exist in authority or decision making responsibility in marriage or ministry in this way of thinking. Mollenkott wrote:

> How would mutual submission work out in a modern marriage? First, there would be no assumption that either partner is always right or is more important spiritually and hence should have the last word. There would be a careful assessment of gifts: whoever is better at finances might take charge of bill-paying, whoever cooks better might do most of the cooking, and so forth. In case of a radical difference of opinion about an important issue, such as whether the family should move to another city, the partners would work out the differences the way friends have worked out such differences for centuries: by discussing pros and cons, by trying to discern which partner's interests are most deeply concerned.[26]

Basically, the equality of human beings signified that individual gifts rather than presumed roles would decide peoples' activities in the home, church, society and the world.

She developed her thought based on several principles she believed were rooted in Scripture.[27] Mollenkott argued that it was important to recognize that the nature of God included both male and female characteristics, therefore requiring that Christians image God as both masculine and feminine.[28] She argued for this based on the fact that Genesis 1:26 says, "God said, 'Let us make man in our image. . . .'" Because this statement included a general term for all of mankind, therefore, when God refers to creating both man and woman in His image, this action means that God also is masculine and feminine.[29] In the Christian way of relating, then, men and women are equal because they were first created in God's image.

She also based her thought on the teachings and actions of Jesus. In *Women, Men, & the Bible* Mollenkott reminded her readers that Jesus was revolutionary in the compassion he showed to women in his day.[30] She wrote, "The more we find out about the cultural conditions of Jesus' day, the more we realize that in situations like the conversation with the Samaritan woman, Jesus was deliberately breaking customs which were degrading to the self-concept of women. He was providing object lessons for his disciples-and for us all."[31] She expanded her thinking accordingly:

> After his resurrection, Jesus deliberately withheld the honor of his first resurrection appearance from John and Peter, who had been at the tomb on Easter

morning, in order to reveal himself to Mary Magdalene. . . . In Jesus' societal context, women were not acceptable as witnesses in a court of law. By those standards, such an important message should have been entrusted only to men. But Jesus very deliberately reserved for Mary the vision of resurrected being and very deliberately entrusted the magnificent resurrection message to her. Once again, Jesus was creating an object lesson for the disciples concerning the full personhood and ministry of women. It is disheartening that after twenty centuries, many Christian churches still reject female ministry, and many Christian men and women still fail to treat women with the full human respect Jesus never failed to show.[32]

According to the feminist tenet that men and women were created equal in personhood and function, Mollenkott's understanding of Jesus' treatment of women supported her presupposition.

She also reinterpreted the traditional understanding of the incarnation to support this belief. She wrote:

Instead the model is that of the Christ in human form giving up self for the church, and the church's submission in response to that self-sacrificial love. So instead of the dominance and submission model, we have a mutual submission model. According to this model or metaphor, the incarnation of Christ for the purpose of dying to redeem the church represents the giving up of the self will of the Christian husband in relation to the wife.[33]

Therefore, the man and woman are equal because of the model of the Trinity. Christ was in nature God submitting to Himself, therefore, the woman only submits to the man because the man has first submitted to his own deepest Self (the Holy Spirit within him), as Jesus did.[34] This change of focus aids her argument that the Christian way of relating is mutual submission because Christ submitted to his own divine self-will, therefore, the man and woman are both to do the same with no real distinction in their roles.[35]

Interestingly for Mollenkott, since her understanding of the creation of men and women included the male and female aspects of God, therefore, the way that one imaged God was affected as well. If the first of "mankind" was created male and female in God's image, then more female imagery in language usage became Mollenkott's next argument. This concern found expression in her book *The Divine Feminine: The Biblical Imagery of God as Female*. In this book, Mollenkott pointed to many biblical passages utilizing female God-images as the basis for her argument that more female imagery should be included in Christian theology.[36] The origins of this argument are based in this feminist belief that the constitution of male/female personhood is equal, so that their roles are dictated by their individual gifts.

Traditional Teachings on Men and Women
Are Rooted in Outdated Patriarchy

Early on in the writings of Virginia Ramey Mollenkott, she argued against the patriarchal attitudes and their contributing effects within the church. The concept of patriarchy largely arose in feminist literature during the 1960s and 1970s.[37] According to feminist theology, patriarchy was used within religion, particularly Christianity, to perpetuate the oppression of women through traditional gender roles.[38] By the time that Mollenkott published *Women, Men, & the Bible,* the concept of patriarchy was well established in all forms of feminist thought. Her adherence to it is considered here.

In the second chapter of *Women, Men, & the Bible* Mollenkott compared what she called the "Christian way of relating" to the "patriarchal way of relating."[39] By this terminology Mollenkott challenged traditional teaching on role relationships. She grounded her argument in the need to overthrow the "Christian heresy" of patriarchalism.[40]

She began this attempt by critiquing the power structure of the church she believed was patriarchal to its core. Fundamental to the stability of this power structure, according to Mollenkott, was traditional hermeneutics. Through these interpretations of the Bible, men remain in powerful positions and women in subordinate positions within the church.[41] It was at this point that Mollenkott's devotion to "new hermeneutics" came into play; however, development of this theme will be considered later in this work. It is important, nonetheless, at this point to notice the connection of these two themes. Mollenkott's devotion to feminism was strengthened by her conviction that patriarchy was an outdated power structure that oppressed women. This oppression was perpetuated by the way that the church used masculine language in their interpretation of the Bible. Therefore, both of these themes were integral in her theology.

The next natural step to take in her argumentation was the issue of language. Since the power structures of Christianity were perpetuated through patriarchalism, central to their methodology to continue the oppression of women was the androcentric language. Historically, the Trinity was referred to as Father, Son, and Holy Spirit. Mollenkott, however, took issue with the images of God as primarily masculine in nature. Therefore, as early in her writings as *Women, Men, & the Bible* she argued for a more inclusive imagery of God.[42] She argued, "I have been forced to realize that the exclusive use of male pronouns concerning God, the association of God with masculinity to the exclusion of femininity, has indeed been the cause of much idolatry."[43] For Mollenkott, patriarchy represented all that was harmful for women; for that reason, everything associated with it should be rejected and avoided.

As Mollenkott's theology expanded in the following two decades, her understanding of the term patriarchy did as well. In her 1978 publication *Is the Homosexual My Neighbor?*, Mollenkott began to address what would become her central theme in later writings, acceptance of gay, lesbian, bisexual, and transsegender people into the Christian church and life.[44] As her thought developed related to this concern, Mollenkott moved away from the term patriarchy to describe the traditional understanding of gender roles as heteropatriarchy. This term described how "male supremacy is maintained by teaching young women that their destiny is to meet the needs of men and by teaching young men that their masculinity depends on gaining control over women. Compulsory heterosexuality is the very backbone that holds patriarchy together."[45] In other words, patriarchy as a descriptor was not broad enough. Mollenkott did not want to address the concerns of male/female roles alone. She wanted to address the changing trends of sexual and gender orientation within culture.[46] Therefore, her acceptance of the critique of patriarchy by feminist thinkers evolved to a critique of traditional understandings of gender and sexuality in general. Her growing theology is evident in this observation.

The New Humanity

Ultimately, feminist thinkers re-envisioned all of society to be a place where men and women co-exist without predetermined roles.[47] For Mollenkott, the terms the "New Humanity" and the "New Creation" became the phrases that described her adherence to this belief. Throughout her lifetime, her feminism changed as did her understanding of the concepts related to its development. Hints of this belief in the New Humanity were evident early on in her writings referring to the mutuality of relating to one another.[48] In *Is the Homosexual My Neighbor?* Mollenkott used the term "co-humanity" to express her belief in this concept. By using this term, she expressed her belief that human beings were created to live and exist together on the earth without relationships of predetermined authority.[49] Subsequently, in her book *Godding: Human Responsibility and the Bible*, Mollenkott fully expanded her ideas on this subject.

She wrote:

> What I am driving at is simple enough, and is the thesis of this book: that human responsibility, in its deepest and fullest dimension, entails godding, an embodiment or incarnation of God's love in human flesh, with the goal of co-creating with God a just and loving human society.[50]

The task of co-creating a just and loving society was the definition of the New Humanity. This society, according to Mollenkott, was just and loving because of the task of each person to "god" or practice loving and accepting other people just as they were created without judgment.[51]

Mollenkott fully acknowledged her proclivity towards inclusivism with her usage of this term. She wrote, "It is my conviction that godding, a conscious cooperation infused with the Holy Spirit, calls us toward an all-inclusive attitude, a theology of the wind, a relationship to God and the world that does not try to make things easy by ruling out whole areas of human experience and whole groups of human beings."[52] The New Humanity was a place where not only men and woman existed together without distinction of prejudice, but also people of every sexual variation could exist without this judgment except for sexual practices that abuse other people. Therefore, Mollenkott's feminist leanings opened her thought for broader expressions of sexuality.

In Mollenkott's view of the New Humanity, the existence of all forms of gender and sexual difference—lesbianism, homosexuality, bisexuality, and all forms of transgender people—can actually operate as social transformers.[53] They play this role in society as people who bravely go against the norm of traditionally acceptable expressions of sexuality and gender. By their very existence, Mollenkott argued, Christians are forced to question their own identity and role in life. As heterosexual people encounter others who have not simply accepted their role in mainstream society, they are challenged to consider their views of other people as they attempt to love and accept them. Therefore, Mollenkott urged people of minority orientations to "come out" as acts of faith for the good of the society, not just their own identity.[54]

Mollenkott's adherence to the concept of the New Humanity blossomed over time. However, she first encountered this term in her early research of feminist theology. In this analysis of the major themes in her thought system, a consideration of this issue would leave the analysis incomplete. In her expanding theological convictions, Mollenkott expressed her allegiance to feminism through her ideas of the equality of men and women; her critique of patriarchal gender roles; and her desire for a New Humanity.

NEW HERMENEUTICAL METHODOLOGY

The third major thematic emphasis of Virginia Ramey Mollenkott to be taken up in this study is her commitment to new hermeneutical methodology. At the time of Mollenkott's emergence in the theological gender debate, non-traditional hermeneutical methods were being employed. Mollenkott, with her doctorate in interpretation of literature made use of the best scholarly methods available to her. She discussed her adherence to them and the reasons for their usage in her writing in *Sensuous Spirituality*:

> Here I want only to explain why I myself switched from the traditional herme-neutics I believed for the first thirty-five years of my life to the pluralistic hermeneutics I have outlined here. In the first place, as a woman (and a *lesbian* woman at that) I was desperate. Like the Greek woman who became creative and assertive because she was desperate for the healing of her daughter, I was desperate for authenticity, for the healing of my self-esteem, and for the use of my gifts. . . . So, the second reason why I switched, however gradually, from a traditionalist to a more inclusive hermeneutic: not only because I was desperate for my own healing, but in response to the normative love ethic that you shall love your neighbor as yourself. Third and finally, I chose the pluralistic herme-neutic because I discovered that it is more honest, contextual, and scholarly than the traditionalist method.[55]

Mollenkott's new hermeneutics are analyzed here.

The Personal Reason for New Hermeneutics: Pursuit of Wholeness

Virginia Ramey Mollenkott experienced several painful experiences as a child as has been previously discussed in this work. By her own admission, these experiences left her trying to reconcile her own pain with the religious teaching she was exposed to as a child in the Plymouth Brethren church. Her search for wholeness left her open, then, to influences from outside the reli-gious background she had known as a child.

A major principle in the newer hermeneutical methods Mollenkott adapted was the validity of human experience as a lens to interpret the Bible.[56] This existential approach appealed to her in a way unlike the religious teaching from her childhood. Repeatedly Mollenkott spoke of being told as a child that God did not love people who were not heterosexual.[57] Therefore, as she studied the concepts of the new hermeneutics this portion of her life could be validated or at least seriously considered outside a spirit of judgmentalism.[58] She wrote:

> So how does a fundamentalist who believes she is essentially and totally depraved become transformed into a person who knows she is an innocent spiritual being who is temporarily having human experiences? The answer is: through a long and gradual process involving the study of hermeneutics; a great deal of dreaming and learning to interpret those dreams; extensive journaling; psychological use of the *I Ching* and the Tarot to learn something

about the movement of my unconscious mind; agonizing struggles with *A Course in Miracles*; studying the works of Paul Norman Tuttle; reading up on the hermetic tradition and on spiritual healing; much pondering of great theological poets like John Milton and Emily Dickinson; listening to and reading outstanding thinkers among my contemporaries; learning how to love and be loved; the experience of my mother's death and thereafter our continued closeness; here and there, some psychotherapy; and some mildly mystical experiences.[59]

Mollenkott believed that a major part of her life's work was to help people be "fully alive."[60] Critical in the experience of being "fully alive" was experiencing peace and harmony in relationships. For Mollenkott, who felt more naturally herself as a lesbian, her source of peace rested in accepting and validating these experiences.[61] Only outdated heteropatriarchy and traditional hermeneutics rejected such lifestyles. Therefore, as she grew in her search for personal wholeness, her movement away from traditional hermeneutics contributed to her development.

The Societal Reason for New Hermeneutics:
A Just and Loving Society

Mollenkott believed that personal wholeness was not complete unless it found expression in the everyday workings of society. If people were to be able to love and be loved in the economy of a fair society, then a revolution had to take place privately and publicly. Therefore, by adhering to her feminist leanings she argued for the New Humanity.[62] The New Humanity, or New Creation, was one where no distinction of authority existed between man and woman, thereby liberating women from their patriarchal oppression. Thus, discovering the language and correct usage of language in the New Creation was central to the establishment of a just and loving society.[63]

Mollenkott's hermeneutics were grounded in the belief that the old power structures of traditionalism were oppressive for women and all people who were not heterosexual white men.[64] Therefore, her new practices were designed to encourage the liberation of women and all oppressed people. Mollenkott argued that the patriarchal culture present in Scripture was no longer applicable for those desiring freedom from patriarchy.[65] Her rejection of passages that supported patriarchy was evidence of her hermeneutical progression. These changes were directly related to her desire for a just and loving society. Only through liberation of all oppressed peoples would this new society come into existence. Therefore, her desire for the New Humanity fueled her disposition toward more progressive hermeneutical practices.

The Central Issue of New Hermeneutics:
The Authority of Scripture

Bernard Ramm, a pioneer in developing newer hermeneutical methods in the twentieth century, wrote:

> Although the Christian ministry is manifold and ought not to be seen exclusively as preaching, without doubt it reaches its fullest expression in the preaching of the Word of God. If this is the nature of the Protestant ministry it follows that one of the most important considerations of the Christian ministry must be the right use of the Word of God.[66]

However, departing from the traditional interpretive methods, Ramm goes on to advocate progressive revelation.[67] By this he means, "The concept of progressive revelation is based upon the conviction that revelation and redemption move along a historical line and that this historical line has a certain character to it."[68] In other words, the revelation given in the Bible occurs chronologically, and heavier emphasis and applicability must be given to that which is revealed later than that which is given earlier. It was at this point that traditional Biblical scholars took issue with the evolving hermeneutical methods of younger evangelicals. For them, the heart of the issue was the authority of all of Scripture, not just what was revealed in the New Testament.

According to Millard Erickson, a prominent systematic theologian,

> All Scripture is historically authoritative, that is, it tells us correctly what God expected or required from specific persons at particular times and places. Some of Scripture is also normatively authoritative. That means that those parts of Scripture are to be applied and obeyed in the same fashion in which they were originally given.[69]

Authority was the issue at stake in the acceptance of the new hermeneutics by all of the younger evangelicals; however, it particularly applied to religious feminists. Because the historical authority of men in leadership in the home and church was the issue being questioned in feminist ideology, the traditional position on the authority of the Bible was also in question. Feminist theologians in the latter twentieth century easily accepted the new hermeneutic because they challenged the understanding of authority in general.

The question of the authority of Scripture is a common critique of the new hermeneutical practices of feminists.[70] The evidence of these new practices occurs throughout all of Mollenkott's books. Several places in her thought where the development and use of them contributed to her theology are considered next in this analysis.

Mollenkott's Women, Men, & the Bible

Mollenkott began her first feminist theological book by stating her allegiance to the Bible, and in chapter 5 she began to critique those who interpreted the Bible using traditional interpretive styles. She wrote, "It is now time to confront squarely the major problems posed by those who deny this position and interpret the Bible in another way."[71]

She argued that traditionalists who use New Testament teachings to require wives to submit to husbands were outdated because the cultural mood had changed since it was originally written.[72] She called this practice the "absolutization of culture." In this practice, the culture of the Bible was not sufficiently considered to determine if its teachings were currently applicable. Traditionalists, in Mollenkott's opinion, simply took all of Scripture to be applicable without careful observation of whether it should be applied to contemporary situations.[73] Mollenkott used this principle to call some of the Apostle Paul's instructions regarding men and women in leadership into question. She was adamant that the culture of the New Testament, especially surrounding the roles of men and women, ruled out the application of these texts to modern contexts.

Later in her book Mollenkott devoted an entire chapter to "learning to interpret accurately."[74] In this portion of the book she identified several basic hermeneutical methods to be appropriated when reading the Bible. She wrote, "The reader must learn to pay attention to the author's choice of words, rhythms, sentence structures, images or word pictures, point of view, and so forth, in order to experience what the work actually embodies."[75] Immediately following this statement Mollenkott questioned the reader as to whether he had realized that the two Genesis accounts of creation were contradictory.[76] Here, Mollenkott's new hermeneutics allowed her to at once write that she held the Bible in high respect and at the same time to question its consistency in teaching. For the traditionalist, this type of interpretive style was unacceptable.

Mollenkott's The Divine Feminine: The Biblical Imagery of God as Female.

Mollenkott continued her use of these practices by developing the concept of female images of God as utilized in the Bible. The implications of this book are many, however, in this section only the fact that she devoted an entire book to revisioning the image of God is considered. First, she wrote, "The only potentially exclusive distinctive that shows up in English grammar is the gender distinction of male, female, or neuter. With relatively little effort, grammar can be manipulated so that females as well as males are included and affirmed."[77] Therefore, the serious student of the Bible ought to adjust their image of God to include the Bible's female images and nature as well as male imagery, and to be inclusive in translating the text in order to be less offensive to men and women. Both of these practices were evidence of the new hermeneutical methodology affirmed by Mollenkott.

Mollenkott's Godding: Human Responsibility and the Bible

In an attempt to lay out her basic approach to biblical interpretation, Mollenkott wrote:

> I approach the Bible not as a specialist in Hebrew or Greek, but simply as a professor of literature in English. I am aware that the Bible was written across many centuries by many different hands, with the Old Testament canon taking a thousand years to be decided. Still, I think there is something to be gained by taking the package as it has been handed down to us and attempting to make sense of it as an organic and living whole. This involves assuming that canonical decisions, however chaotic they may have been, nevertheless had some wisdom to them. Using this approach, let me try to demonstrate my conviction that the Bible is a liberating and empowering book for modern women as well as men.[78]

While Mollenkott stated that she wanted to approach the Bible with respect and authority, she still came to it with her presupposition that it would "liberate" people, women especially. She went on to encourage the serious study of biblical languages, literature, and culture even though she never formally engaged in such scholarship.

Furthering her example of the need to study biblical contexts, Mollenkott cited the use of the word *kephale* in New Testament Greek.[79] In this argument, she disputed the traditional interpretation of *kephale* to mean "head" by citing outside biblical sources to support its meaning as "source." Mollenkott concluded this section by stating that the biblical student must be careful not to disrespect the biblical "authors understandings of words within their own cultural experience."[80] Hence, Mollenkott cited research in cultural background as support for her interpretation of the word *kephale* rather than accepting the traditionalist interpretation for the word.

"Another old and respected hermeneutical principle is this one: that difficult, obscure, and highly unusual biblical passages must never be used to govern the interpretation of clearer more common themes."[81] She then mentioned the usage of 1 Timothy 2:11–15 to prohibit women teaching men in the church. According to Mollenkott's newer understanding of this older interpretive concept, since the teaching in 1 Timothy is "quirky," it should not be used to contradict other more liberating passages of Scripture. She also cited evidence that the teaching in 1 Timothy was largely culturally relevant at the time of its writing, so application for the twentieth century was inappropriate.

Mollenkott concluded this section of her book *Godding: Human Responsibility and the Bible* by urging a:

> Return to serious Bible study that pays attention to historical context and to the flow of ideas, images, and grammar within chapters and books and indeed pays attention to the whole overarching structure of the Hebrew and Christian Scriptures taken as a unit.[82]

Virginia Ramey Mollenkott, from her very first book, was honest and open about her adherence to the new hermeneutical practices of her time. The theme is easily observed in her thoughts and in the progression of her theology. She expressed her struggles with her pursuit for wholeness that influenced her questioning of traditional hermeneutical practices. The personal conviction of loyalty to the Bible's sufficiency remained throughout her writings, although she was also influenced by New Age practices, social science research, and contemporary culture. These resources consistently comply with new hermeneutical methodology, thus it remained a strong theme throughout her writing.

NEW UNDERSTANDING OF SOTERIOLOGY

Along with Mollenkott's new hermeneutics and feminism came the reinterpretation of many of her metaphysical beliefs. In her chapter in *Women of Faith in Dialogue*, Mollenkott wrote:

> Partly to counterbalance my own early fundamentalist training, I now place great stress on the liberating implications of the Gospel. Through a long spiritual evolution I have become convinced that the *evangelium*, the Good News, is biblically intended to be Good News to all the oppressed and wretched of the earth by turning people of faith into agents of peace and justice. True to my evangelical roots, I have found the Bible itself has been my chief radicalizer.[83]

Specifically, Mollenkott's understanding of salvation changed as she shifted from her traditional beliefs to her feminist beliefs, ultimately pushing her towards universalism.

Mollenkott's Feminist Definition of Salvation

In feminist theology, traditional views of sin and salvation are redefined in order to argue for freedom from oppression from patriarchal expectations. This particular belief arose from a commitment to liberation theology and its adjustment to Western society. Mollenkott's acceptance of feminism affected her understanding of salvation. Treated next in this chapter are the two major reasons for her change: commitment to liberation theology and salvation as freedom from patriarchal oppression.

The Influence of Liberation Theology

Feminism, at its core ideologically, was heavily influenced by liberation theology.[84] Religious feminists, in particular, were fond of its message of freedom from oppressive power structures.[85] Ultimately this sort of thinking led to redefining the traditional meanings of sin and salvation. Understanding basic tenets of this theology is helpful in grasping Mollenkott's change in her soteriology.

Freedom from oppression for any minority people in a society or circumstance is considered to be salvation in liberation theology.[86] Mollenkott exhibited her agreement with this concept in *Women, Men, & the Bible* when she argued that the "Christian way of relating" was that of mutual submission, thereby demolishing all traditional gender roles.[87] Sin, consequently, is understood as anything that prolongs this oppression and others and perpetuates the power structures which force oppression.[88] Liberation theology developed in Latin American settings where people experienced struggles within corrupt governmental settings; however, feminist scholars studied these concepts and applied them to gender roles in the West.[89]

Influence of this thinking can be observed through her statements in several of her books. She wrote:

> Traditionally, sin has been defined as selfish pride. . . . This seems a very accurate definition of sin when applied to those who are either financially or physically stronger and thus normative over others. But when it is preached by a dominant group to subordinate groups, it becomes an ugly distortion of reality. Every attempt the subordinates make to achieve greater autonomy is interpreted by the normative group as selfish pride—despite the fact the subordinates are merely trying to attain a status the "normatives" already possess.[90]

Later in that book, she elaborated more her understanding of sin. She wrote, "I would like to clarify that I recognize evil as a force to struggle against tirelessly if we are speaking about personal alienation or about the oppressive systems of racism, sexism, classicism, heterosexism, and the like."[91] In Mollenkott's discussion of her views of sin and salvation, her loyalty to feminism and its implications, clearly influenced her theological development.

Salvation as Freedom from Patriarchal Oppression

Mollenkott believed and wrote passionately of the need for the freedom of women from patriarchal oppression. To some extent, salvation itself took on this meaning as she became more and more convinced of this need for all American women, both inside and outside the church. As her theological allegiances grew away from her extreme fundamental background, the new definition of sin and salvation developed along the lines of her feminist beliefs. Growth in her thought is observed through the consideration of several of her own quotes.

In her chapter on "Bible Doctrines and Human Equality" from *Women, Men, & the Bible* she portrayed her new understanding of the Genesis accounts. She wrote, "The first time dominance and submission enter into the male-female relationships is after the fall. Genesis 3:14–19 pronounces a curse on the serpent and a curse on the ground, because of sin."[92] Therefore, Mollenkott alluded to the fact that hierarchy in male-female relationships was due to sin, and actually became the sin that perpetuated this hierarchy in life after the fall. After describing the way society has transcended men's earning food by the sweat of their brows, she commented on sin's result that, "And for another, men will exert dominance over their wives. . . . But interestingly enough, there has been no concerted effort to overcome the tendency of males to dominate females. There is no shocked outcry from the Christian world when Christian husbands act domineering or Christian wives act manipulative."[93] By elaborating on the effects of the fall, Mollenkott demonstrated her belief that the essence of sin was the existence of hierarchical relationships, therefore the power struggle and manipulation involved in them.

She also expanded her view of salvation as the freedom from patriarchal oppression in *Godding*. She wrote:

> For instance, many American women in recent decades have realized that their claims to individualism (in an individualistic culture) have been denied 'on behalf of biological or spiritual determinism that relegates [women] to the realm of nature rather than autonomous will.' For this reason, feminist aspirations often take a highly individualistic form, and religious pundits have been quick to label those aspirations shamefully selfish. But the fact is that having internationalized society's relegation of them to natural determinism, these same women had tended to consider everybody's needs *except* their own.[94]

Women in America, in other words, had been socialized to accept their status as wives and mothers that they were not even able to claim their full personhood According to this line of reasoning Mollenkott further illustrated her belief in sin as patriarchal oppression and salvation as freedom from this oppression. Her commitment to feminist theological principles led to focusing on questions related to the exclusive claims of Christ for salvation. These views are considered next.

Mollenkott's Universalist View of Salvation

According to Millard Erickson, a universalist soteriology is one that basically asserts that "all will be saved" regardless on their belief system or way of life.[95] There are varieties of belief universalists, however, the common denominator in them is this conviction that somehow every person will be saved from eternal judgment. Mollenkott, in her later years, demonstrated a move toward this type of soteriology.

The Influence of Ecumenism

During her time working on the committee for the Inclusive Language Lectionary for the National Council of Churches and engaged in interreligious dialogue at the American Jewish Committee, Mollenkott came into contact with women from many faith traditions. She credits this time of her life to causing her to question her belief in exclusive salvation through Jesus Christ alone.[96] As she grew to value interreligious dialogue, she began to doubt that all people outside the Christian faith would be condemned. She wrote, "As for our Muslim sisters and brothers, we need only remind ourselves of God's tender concern for outcast Hagar and Ishmael, as recorded in Genesis 21:8–21."[97] However, while this thought correctly points out that God did consider the outcast, Mollenkott understood it to mean that they would eventually be included in salvation. This interpretation is her understanding of what the text means when it said that God was "with Ishmael."

She also revealed her changing definition of salvation through statements on universal redemption. She wrote:

> And as we have seen, some prophets from both Judaism and Christianity have specifically envisioned a redemption that reaches to people of faith beyond the confines of their own tradition. Their vision seems to me a good paradigm for interreligious dialogue: each of us maintaining loyalty to the external forms of our own religious, yet willing to share an inner experience and universal outreach with people whose external forms differ significantly from our own. Although each of us may secretly nourish the expectation that when the Day of God is fully revealed, everyone else will be brought into the fold we ourselves already inhabit, fortunately this is not a matter that has to be settled while we are sharers together of the ambiguous human condition.[98]

In this statement, Mollenkott expressed her belief that it was acceptable to practice what-ever religion one found meaningful, and at the end of time perhaps they would all be included "in the fold" regardless of their life or convictions. Her growing commitment to free all oppressed people through her work with women of all faiths influenced her definition of salvation.

Mollenkott's soteriology progressed throughout the development of her career in thought and practice. Understanding salvation was central to her theological development because of her search for personal healing. However, through time her commitment to feminist ideas and ecumenical practices altered her traditional evangelical view of salvation. Cultural issues that played crucial roles in the movement and themes of her theology are considered next in this chapter.

CULTURAL ISSUES

Mollenkott began and developed her career on the basis of concern over certain culturally relevant issues. In this sense, she was truly a "younger evangelical," or a person who believed that the church for too long had ignored the social challenges of society in general.[99] The two most relevant emphases in the development of her theology were homosexuality and inclusive language. Both of these topics are treated here for their place in the development of the themes in Mollenkott's theology.

Homosexuality

The focus that began as concern for the equal treatment of women in the late 1970s eventually led to a concern for the equal treatment of homosexual people and all gender variants. Mollenkott was convinced that this was the ultimate calling of her career. So much so that she called for a radical revisioning of all of society and especially the church.[100]

Accepting the Homosexual Who is One's Neighbor

Mollenkott argued that the Christian church was basically defunct in its ministry to homosexual people. In her analysis, the church should be the place for homosexuals to find healing and acceptance from the many trials they face. This type of discussion appeared early on in her co-authored book, *Is the Homosexual My Neighbor?* published in 1978. Much controversy surrounded its publication because of the radical ideas presented within it by Mollenkott and Scanzoni.

Accepting the Homosexuality of One's Neighbor

However, Mollenkott and Scanzoni did not stop at a call for the equal treatment of homosexuals, but argued for acceptance of this lifestyle based on the need for compassion. They did not just believe that the church should step up to minister to the needs of homosexuals, but that Christians should condone this sexual preference. They believed that any expression of responsible sexuality should be tolerated by the church based on the concern for being both biblical and loving in nature. They believed as Christians developed their moral sensibilities, their acceptance of homosexuality broadened as well.[101] Those believers who were actually growing, in other words, were the ones who were alert and aware of this need in popular culture of the ministry of acceptance to homosexuals. Therefore, people who were the most spiritually aware of the progression in culture were also the ones who were the most morally mature.[102]

Accepting Life Beyond Gender Categories:
Transgender Realities

As Mollenkott matured in her theological development she became more critical of what she called the binary gender construct.[103] Most dualisms in Mollenkott's theology were considered unacceptable; therefore, the male/female gender dualism was no different.[104] She argued that too many injustices had occurred because of the understanding that masculine and feminine roles are radically different.[105] Therefore, all predetermined role distinctions should cease and the result should be an omni-gendered society.

A society in which predetermined role distinctions between males or females existed, and in which in-between identities were also accepted, would be an omnigender society. Every person, man, woman, and child, would be free to express their own gender and sexual orientations.[106] In fact, the more confusing the gender choices, the more difficult to distinguish one's gender, the more the individual might have to struggle to achieve authenticity.[107] Mollenkott believed that to establish a truly free society, no predetermined gender roles should be forced upon anyone. Therefore, all gender-based biases would be eliminated and the New Creation would be ushered into existence.

Inclusive Language

The next major cultural trend that Mollenkott took up was the question of inclusive language. If the progressive revelation of God had moved toward accepting a more egalitarian society, the language of this culture ought to support human equality. In fact, in Mollenkott's reasoning, not only should it describe this culture, language usage should also be a part of ushering in the new society, or the New Creation. Therefore, inclusive language, or language devoid of gender biases, became Mollenkott's next major concern. As early on as her first book, *Women, Men, & the Bible,* she commented on this need, and as time went on inclusive language only grew in importance to her. The concept was fully developed in *The Divine Feminine: The Biblical Imagery of God as Female* published in 1983. Three aspects of this thematic development are considered here: language denoting equal treatment for men and women; language for God Himself; and language for the New Creation as a whole.

Language for the Equality of Men and Women

In *Women, Men, & the Bible*, Mollenkott began arguing for inclusive language usage. She developed all of chapter five into "Is God Masculine?" In this chapter, she attributed the exclusive usage of masculine God language to idolatry of the male in traditional hierarchical relationships. She wrote:

> During the last several years, radical feminists have been saying that if God is male, then male is God. I had very little sympathy for such statements until I began to read the various attacks on equal-partnership marriage which were discussed in chapter 2. Reading them, I have been forced to realize that the exclusive use of male pronouns concerning God, the association of God with masculinity to the exclusion of femininity, has indeed been the cause of much idolatry.[108]

She believed that the overwhelming masculine imagery in language used in the Bible was understandable at the time of its writing, but in exclusive use in contemporary society was harmful to women and human relationships. Therefore, she argued for a change in emphasis to include both masculine and feminine nouns and pronouns.

Her belief that this language usage should change was rooted in her argument for mutual submission in marriage.[109] By arguing for masculine and feminine language usage she hoped to encourage more receptivity to her concept of equal partnership in marriage. Mollenkott hoped that this relationship model would replace the headship/ submission model that she believed promoted patriarchy. She thought that to use masculine terms only for God meant thinking of God as only masculine.[110] Thus, idolatry of men was encouraged because of the close association of God and men in language usage. Therefore, she began to develop her argument for word imagery that directly described God. She wrote, "It becomes obvious that speaking of God in exclusively masculine terms can create tragic confusion, even in the minds of intelligent people."[111]

Language for God

To alleviate this confusion, then, Mollenkott began to support imagery that alluded to an androgynous concept of God.[112] She wrote that since God transcends all sexuality anyway, language that refers to him/her should communicate this idea. She believed that inclusive language used to refer to God or about God was the best way to refer to Him. In the development of Mollenkott's theology, this emphasis was the beginning of creating a better society for both men and women. Therefore, she devoted an entire book to this topic. In this book Mollenkott argued that:

> It seems natural to assume that Christian people, eager to transmit the Good News that the Creator loves each human being equally and unconditionally, would be right in the vanguard of those who utilize inclusive language. Yet a visit to almost any church on Sunday morning indicates that alas, it is not happening that way. Whereas a "secular" publisher like McGraw-Hill has insisted on inclusive language for almost a decade, the language of Christian preaching, prayer and hymnody is still laden with exclusive-sounding references to men, man, brothers, sons and the God of Abraham, Isaac, and Jacob.[113]

Her argument, clearly observed in this quote, was based on her cultural concern that language for God would not only affect Christian, but also popular culture.

She argued that the Christian church had largely neglected the many feminine images of God in the Bible, and therefore contributed to patriarchal oppression of women.[114] By reinterpreting at least fifteen images for God found in the Bible, then, Mollenkott began to correct this problem. These expositions of biblical imagery included God as a female pelican, God as a Homemaker, and God as Mother Bear. Each of these images was portrayed as a unique symbol that allowed men and women to get more in touch with the feminine side of God.

In the conclusion of this book, Mollenkott honestly admitted that, "When all is said and done, the Bible contains massively more masculine God-language and male God-imagery than female imagery."[115] However, she disregarded any real significance in the vast number of masculine imagery because of the patriarchal culture in which the Bible was written.[116] In her understanding of the progressive nature of revelation, however, she believed that central to overcoming patriarchy was constant attention to the Bible, and the change in language usage to refer to God to create the New Humanity. Therefore, Mollenkott argued convincingly for the urgent need to change language to ensure equal treatment for men, women, God and ultimately all of reality.

Language for the New Creation

As Mollenkott's theological themes developed, her strong belief in the coming of the New Humanity fueled the use of inclusive language. She often wrote about the power of language to effect change in reality. Therefore, as her concept of what the New Creation would look like matured, so did her argument for inclusive language.

By the time she wrote *Omnigender* she argued for language to represent a gender-ambivalent society. In her opinion, a society of many expressions of gender was to be encouraged and preferred. Language, then, would help to usher this society into existence. The role of inclusive language became central to the development of the New Creation. She wrote, describing language usage in the New Creation:

> Language too would shift away from binary pronouns (his/her) toward gender-inclusive wording. . . . Although language modulates constantly, individual proposals are usually not the way change occurs. I suspect we may eventually use the plural forms they, them, and their to replace binary singulars, as I have been doing here and there in this book. That was sometimes done in early modern English (Shakespeare's English), and the tendency has constantly reasserted itself ("everybody should turn in their papers now"), even though deemed incorrect by prescriptive grammarians.[117]

Ultimately, the point is language affects the way people think; therefore their beliefs are influenced; subsequently, their actions. So, if Mollenkott wanted to change society to include and accept all forms of gender variety, then she had to affect the language used to refer to that gender variety. In *Transgender Journeys* she asked this question:

> The institutional church and its individual members must honestly consider and respond to the following question: Do we represent the love of Christ to those who are different, or are we merely demanding their conformity to our arbitrary norms in terms of dress and behavior so we can feel more comfortable and save ourselves potential dis-ease or awkwardness?[118]

Mollenkott went on to identify the use of language as a vital part of changing the largely heterosexual culture to include all forms of gender variance as the cultural norm. In her opinion, as the language of a culture goes, so goes the culture. Since the goal for Mollenkott was to transform society, the coming of the New Creation depended on the language used in that culture.

Homosexuality and inclusive language, for Mollenkott, were theological themes driven by her concern for relevance in popular culture. Her commitment to these two issues was clear throughout her writing. Interesting in the development of all of her theological themes, but especially these two cultural issues, is the interplay of the relationship between the themes. As her commitment to one grew, so did the importance of the other topic. In the conclusion of this critical analysis of Mollenkott's feminist theology more attention is given to this point; however observation of this fact in her thematic development is worth acknowledging here.

The Need for Analysis

Ultimately, Mollenkott's theology grew over time as her commitment to each of the listed themes expanded and opened to other themes. The influence of her concerns along with her emphasis on biblical authority in interaction with reason and experience took Mollenkott on a different road than the one she began on in her childhood. However, studying her theological position is important to gain a clearer understanding of all of her views and major themes within her theology. Mollenkott believed that a kind of subversion was called for in order to overthrow Christian patriarchy. In *Sensuous Spirituality* she wrote, "Subversion means a systematic attempt to overthrow or undermine a political system by persons who work secretly within the system involved."[119] Without reservation or apology, Mollenkott worked from within the Christian faith to undermine certain traditional teachings on the nature, meaning, and significance of sexuality and gender. Throughout her public ministry, a continual movement can be observed in her theological commitments. What can be learned from her movement? Are there any indications for the reasons behind her movements? These are the questions at the heart of this study. Chapter five will conclude with an internal and external critique of Mollenkott's thought.

CONCLUSION

I am aware that some of my readers may be thinking that I have deserted Christianity in favor of the new metaphysics. But I would ask them this: can you be certain that I am not being drawn back to the essence of what Jesus actually believed, lived, and taught?[120]

Throughout the development of Mollenkott's theology her ideas progressed little by little. Her early academic experiences caused her to discover Christian humanism; from there, she encountered feminism. This commitment to feminism led to a national ministry eventually introducing her to concerns of hermeneutical methodology, soteriology, and cultural issues. Mollenkott's involvement in these areas within evangelicalism brought her national attention and influence. The role of each of these themes in her theology is considered next in this study.

NOTES

1. Virginia Ramey Mollenkott, *Adamant and Stone Chips: A Christian Humanist Approach Knowledge* (Waco, TX: Word, 1967), 22.
2. Ibid., 16.

3. Ibid.

4. Ibid., 42.

5. Virginia Ramey Mollenkott, *In Search of Balance* (Waco, TX: Word, 1969), 30.

6. Virginia R. Mollenkott, *Speech, Silence, Action! The Cycle of Faith* (Nashville: Abingdon, 1980), 31.

7. Mollenkott, *Adamant and Stone Chips*, 12.

8. Virginia R. Mollenkott, *Sensuous Spirituality: Out from Fundamentalism* (New York: Crossroad, 1993), 110.

9. Mollenkott, *Speech, Silence, Action!*, 23.

10. Virginia R. Mollenkott and Vanessa Sheridan, *Transgender Journeys* (Cleveland: Pilgrim, 2003), 45.

11. Mollenkott, *Sensuous Spirituality*, 189.

12. Mollenkott, *Adamant and Stone Chips*, 12.

13. William Franklin and Joseph M. Shaw, *The Case for Christian Humanism* (Grand Rapids: W. B. Eerdmans, 1991), 4.

14. Ibid., 13.

15. Mollenkott, *In Search of Balance*, 13.

16. Ibid.

17. Mollenkott, *Adamant and Stone Chips*, 15.

18. Mollenkott and Sheridan, *Transgender Journeys*, 42.

19. Mollenkott's developing idea of the unified vision can be seen in many of her books. However, in *Speech, Silence, Action!* she specifically speaks of her encounter with mysticism as an influence for her accepting other religious experiences as valid, thereby broadening her understanding of the unified vision. Cited in Mollenkott, *Speech, Silence, Action!*, 102.

20. Ibid., 23.

21. Ibid., 26.

22. Ibid., 27.

23. Ibid.

24. Ibid.

25. Virginia R. Mollenkott, *Women, Men, & the Bible* (Nashville: Abingdon, 1977), x.

26. Ibid., 25.

27. Ibid., 42.

28. Ibid., 43.

29. Later Mollenkott developed this idea by stating that the first man was a hermaphrodite in her book *Omnigender* published in 2001 (p. 90). Here, however, Mollenkott's thought is only based on the creation of man and woman expressed in the general term "mankind." Both trains of thought come from her emphasis that man and woman were created in the image of God, which conversely means He is in their image as male and female. As cited in: Mollenkott, *Women, Men, & the Bible*, 43.

30. Ibid., 4.

31. Ibid., 5.

32. Ibid., 10.

33. Ibid., 104.

34. Ibid.

35. It is interesting to note that here Mollenkott addresses the concern of imaging God as too immanent which leads to pantheism. In this account, Mollenkott only addresses the need to be careful in relating to God as one who is only "out there" because it prevents understanding God the way that she wants her reader to view the incarnation. However, in her later book, *Godding*, Mollenkott fully expands this line of reasoning to say that God is in us and we are one with God although God is also above us (transcendent). Cited in Mollenkott, *Women, Men, & the Bible*, 107.

36. Virginia R. Mollenkott, *The Divine Feminine: Biblical Imagery of God as Female* (New York: Crossroad, 1983), 2.

37. Mary Kassian, *The Feminist Mistake* (Wheaton, IL: Crossway, 2005), 27.

38. Adrienne Rich, *Of Women Born* (New York: Bantam, 1976), 57–58.

39. Mollenkott, *Women, Men, & the Bible*, 23.

40. Ibid., ix.

41. Ibid., 24.

42. Ibid., 39.

43. Ibid.

44. Virginia R. Mollenkott and Letha Scanzoni, *Is the Homosexual My Neighbor?* (San Francisco: Harper and Row, 1978), 6.

45. Mollenkott, *Sensuous Spirituality*, 12.

46. Ibid., 13.

47. Anne Carr, "Is Christian Feminist Theology Possible?" *Theological Studies* 43, no. 2 (June 1982): 279.

48. Mollenkott, *Women, Men, & the Bible*, 22.

49. Mollenkott, *Is the Homosexual My Neighbor?* 149.

50. Virginia R. Mollenkott, *Godding: Human Responsibility and the Bible* (New York: Crossroad, 1987), 2.

51. Ibid., 4.

52. Ibid., 39.

53. Ibid., 152.

54. Mollenkott and Sheridan, *Transgender Journeys*, 144.

55. Mollenkott, *Sensuous Spirituality*, 68–69.

56. Bernard Ramm, ed., *Hermeneutics* (Grand Rapids: Baker, 1971), 136.

57. Malkmus, *Lgbtran—Oral History Project.*

58. Mollenkott, *Sensuous Spirituality*, 16.

59. Ibid.

60. Ibid., 72.

61. Ibid., 73.

62. Mollenkott, *Godding*, 16.

63. Mollenkott, *Sensuous Spirituality*, 73.

64. Mollenkott, *Sensuous Spirituality*, 12.

65. Virginia R. Mollenkott, *Women of Faith in Dialogue* (New York: Crossroad, 1987), 107.

66. Ramm, *Hermeneutics*, 5.

67. Ibid., 21.

68. Ibid.

69. Millard J. Erickson, *Christian Theology* (Grand Rapids: Baker, 1988), 267.

70. Pamela Cochran, *Evangelical Feminism: A History* (New York: New York University Press, 2005), 17.

71. Mollenkott, *Women, Men, & the Bible*, 73.

72. Ibid., 74.

73. Ibid.

74. Ibid., 88.

75. Ibid., 89.

76. Ibid., 90.

77. Mollenkott, *The Divine Feminine*, 1.

78. Mollenkott, *Godding*, 97.

79. Ibid., 98.

80. Ibid., 100.

81. Ibid., 104.

82. Ibid., 108.

83. Mollenkott, *Women of Faith in Dialogue*, 63. See also Mollenkott's essay in Ann Braude, *Transforming the Faith of our Fathers: Women Who Changed American Religion* (Palgrave/Macmillan, 2004), where the entire thesis concerns the way she was radicalized by the Bible. This essay is a longer version of the speech she delivered at Harvard University's Conference on Women and Religion in 2002.

84. Kassian, *The Feminist Mistake*, 61.

85. Rosemary Radford Ruether, *Liberation Theology: Human Hope Confronts Christian History and American Power* (New York: Paulist Press, 1972), 1.

86. Ibid., 9.

87. Mollenkott, *Women, Men, & the Bible*, 13.

88. Ruether, *Liberation Theology*, 10.

89. Ibid.

90. Mollenkott, *Godding*, 83–84.

91. Ibid., 138–39.

92. Mollenkott, *Women, Men, & the Bible*, 111.

93. Ibid.

94. Mollenkott, *Godding*, 84.

95. Erickson, *Christian Theology*, 1025.

96. Mollenkott, *Women of Faith in Dialogue*, 64.

97. Ibid., 66.

98. Ibid., 67.

99. Cochran, *Evangelical Feminism*, 8.

100. Mollenkott and Sheridan, *Transgender Journeys*, 51.

101. Ibid., 12.

102. Ibid.

103. Mollenkott, *Omnigender,* vii.

104. Ibid., 3.

105. Ibid., 18.

106. Ibid., 166.

107. Ibid., 168.
108. Mollenkott, *Women, Men, & the Bible,* 39.
109. Ibid., 40.
110. Ibid.
111. Ibid., 42.
112. Ibid., 45.
113. Mollenkott, *The Divine Feminine*, 1–2.
114. Ibid., 5.
115. Ibid., 110.
116. Ibid.
117. Mollenkott, *Omnigender*, 169.
118. Mollenkott and Sheridan, *Transgender Journeys,* 152.
119. Mollenkott, *Sensuous Spirituality*, 48.
120. Ibid., 26.

Chapter Five

Critique of Feminist Theology

Much debate occurred with the response of Evangelicals for Social Action to the relevant cultural concerns for women in the mid-twentieth century. Since that initial phase of discussion many opinions and views have arisen in the evangelical community. As one of the earliest evangelicals to embrace feminist thought, Virginia Mollenkott has been on the forefront of the gender debate, inside and outside evangelicalism. From the perspective of an evangelical, several questions arise from her thought, both from those who embraced feminist leanings and those who did not. Wherever one stands in regard to the feminist viewpoint, Mollenkott's ideas are significant to understand as one of the first influential thinkers in this discussion.

After synthesizing the feminist theology of Mollenkott, this chapter will evaluate her thought. Her belief in Christian humanism, feminism, new hermeneutics, and new soteriology are looked at in this portion of the study. Further analysis and questions related to her logic will be considered through her books and public career. Primarily, attention is given to the implications of her development related to evangelical theology. Mollenkott acknowledged her connection to the evangelical community, but her ideas grew outside of this belief structure. Questions arise around this desire and its fulfilled reality through analysis of her thoughts. What was at stake in her progressing feminist theology? How did Mollenkott acknowledge and work to address any growing tensions? What difference did they make in how she developed, or did not? These questions drive this analysis.

CHRISTIAN HUMANISM:
PRACTICE AND INTERPRETATION

Mollenkott strongly advocated Christian humanism in her first published book *Adamant and the Stone Chips* in 1967. A holistic approach to the arts and literature was attractive to Mollenkott through the works of authors such as C. S. Lewis and J. R. R. Tolkien. As she grew in intellectual acumen, their ideas attempting to reconcile human endeavor with divine purposes offered her an opportunity to integrate new ideas into her early fundamentalism. However some unacknowledged tensions surfaced for Mollenkott. These questions are addressed here.

HUMAN EXPERIENCE AND PRACTICE

In *Speech, Silence, Action!* Mollenkott wrote:

> It is difficult for people who have not known a fundamentalist background to believe the basic, almost primitive struggles such a background can generate in fundamentalist persons as they become educated. What I deeply appreciate from my own background is that I was thoroughly grounded in the surface facts (the words themselves) of the Bible. For that I feel grateful to my mother and to various brothers at the Plymouth Brethren Assemblies.[1]

Though Mollenkott expressed gratitude for some aspects of her upbringing, her religious practices and experiences eventually diverged from her early Plymouth Brethren beliefs. In *Sensuous Spirituality* Mollenkott referred to her childhood religion as being "judgmental and divisive."[2] Her acceptance of the validity of dreams and New Age spirituality were contradictory to traditional evangelical practice. However, she never clearly addressed the extent to which they were inconsistent with her early beliefs. She stated only that they had an impact on her worldview, and that she was grateful for them.

Two examples of these outside influences were the role of dreams and a psychological/spiritual study called *A Course in Miracles*. Commenting on the impact that a dream had on her decision to become a part of the Evangelical Women's Caucus, Mollenkott wrote:

> My 'journey into silence' began, I think, with a very significant dream. I was walking in a city, in a small brick square at the front of a cathedral. On the steps of the cathedral, which was just to my right, stood an angel with golden eyelids, looking at me with infinitely tender loving-kindness. The angel wore a white robe, but I do not remember any wings or halo or even an aura, just those golden eyelids. I had a distinct impression of androgyny, however, and I

was certain that this was an angel and that he/she took a loving interest in my welfare, although no words were spoken. . . . Not long after the dream, I had, in fact, identified myself first with the Evangelical Women's Caucus, where women struggled for power to become all they were meant to be, and then with Evangelicals Concerned, a national task force of homosexuals and heterosexuals working together for a better understanding of homosexuality in the Christian community.[3]

Also, at the urging of a friend Mollenkott began to study New Age spirituality through a book called *A Course in Miracles*. Through this study, Mollenkott credited her growth in understanding the role of the human spirit in her experiences.[4] However, she never fully addressed the contradictory nature of these influences as opposed to her Plymouth Brethren roots. To think critically of her thought structure, this question cannot be avoided: if the Plymouth Brethren approach was, in fact, problematic, why did she not bother to attempt reconciliation of those beliefs with her changing theology?

HUMAN EXPERIENCE AND INTERPRETATION

In her argument for Christian humanism, Mollenkott stated that human ideas and therefore interpretations of these ideas were temporal, not eternal. She stated, "Ideas and causes are temporal, but people are eternal. To mistreat a human being because his ideas differ from mine is thus to harm an eternal being because of a temporal, ephemeral matter."[5] She based these conclusions on the thirteenth chapter of First Corinthians where the Apostle Paul defines love in the context of the Body of Christ. She placed more emphasis on love and the way that it is played out in human relationships than emphasis on beliefs or the possibility of knowing objective reality while here on earth in human condition. "In eternity, man's little partial truths will be forgotten things as he sees reality 'whole face to face;' but the way he has treated his fellow human beings will be forever with him, surely an important factor in the judgment of his works."[6] In other words, Mollenkott believed that ideas are temporary and subject to change, so that the only real indication of epistemological certainty was the way in which one related to others. That, in the end, was all that mattered, since no one could distinguish right beliefs from wrong beliefs with absolute certainty.

To accept Mollenkott's arguments for Christian humanism is to accept a different understanding of biblical hermeneutics from traditional evangelicalism. By affirming the interpretive communities approach of Stanley Fish, Mollenkott indicated her progressive theology.[7] Collective meaning for a group of people became the indicator of truth within each community according to this approach.[8] Therefore, the meaning of the authority of Scripture for Mollenkott changed from the traditional understanding of authority.

Appreciation for the arts, literature, and human endeavor in general were facets of Christian humanism. Applying these ideas to her evangelical beliefs affected her religious practices and interpretive methods. The question at this point in an evaluation of her thought is why she did not address the tension these changes introduced in dialogue with her early theology. They were acknowledged, but never explored for the tensions they represented.

Feminism: Language and Equality

The issue of the degree to which Mollenkott remains in the evangelical community of belief, if at all, must be addressed. Many feminists dispute the viability of integrating feminism into Christianity completely. With the split of the Evangelical Woman's Caucus and the forming of Christians for Biblical Equality, this question became more vital for Mollenkott. She remained a member of the EWC, which also moved theologically towards a more inclusive membership. From the very beginning of her encounter with feminist theology, Mollenkott accepted the influence of those both inside and outside the evangelical community. Furthermore, she acknowledged on several occasions that she considered herself at best to be somewhere along the fringes of that community. In both *Women, Men, & the Bible* and *Is the Homosexual My Neighbor?* she openly criticized the evangelical church. She also increasingly advocated dialogue with those outside of evangelicalism.

FEMINISM: LANGUAGE

One aspect that Mollenkott included in her evangelical feminist theology was an argument for the acceptance of feminine God images and inclusive language. In *Women, Men, & the Bible*, Mollenkott argued that masculine God language lent itself to worship of men in Western society.[9] Therefore, she wanted evangelicals to accept feminine language for God alongside the usual masculine language in order to secure growing social status for women in the church and society. In Mollenkott's growing feminism, God was to be considered both he and she, male and female both and perhaps neither, since God is Spirit. Hence, language describing God took on this same androgynous form. She fully developed this line of thought in *The Divine Feminine: The Biblical Imagery of God as Female*.

Mollenkott believed that feminine language for God would undergird the process of liberation for women. Its usage increased in importance for Mollenkott as her career progressed. The question is how this consistently integrated into her evangelical beliefs. These aspects did not then, nor today, comfortably fit into evangelical theology. The tension of this reality in her ideas is significant to acknowledge and question in analysis.

FEMINISM: EQUALITY

What truly is a just and loving society? This question is at the heart of what Mollenkott asked evangelical theologians to clarify and consider. From her earliest writing, Mollenkott argued for the establishment of a just and loving society, or the New Creation.[10] She wrote, "For too long Christian leaders have blocked genuine friendship between men and women by insisting on a pattern of dominance and submission rather than responding to the liberating message of the Good News."[11] She went on to state that to embrace true friendship was to envision the New Humanity where no predeterimined role distinction exists between men and women. This egalitarian society was the ultimate loving and peaceful place for both men and women, with the absolution of all hierarchy between males and females.

However, the tension for Mollenkott was that she believed she remained within Christian orthodoxy, while at the same time redefining traditional paradigms. Genesis 1 states that "In the beginning God created. . ." every aspect of creation: the earth, the skies, all animals, the seas, and man and woman. Intrinsic in historical Christianity is the argument that God created the world along with all manner of variety in creation. Therefore, sex differences and distinctions are traditionally appreciated in evangelical theology. Ultimately, in the teaching that God created humanity as male and female, there are certain differences implied in their creation.

Mollenkott, throughout her career, argued for a society without predetermined sex role distinctions. She also maintained that her theological position, while altered through the years, was not developed without acute attention to Scripture. She wrote, "The biblical images of God as natural phenomena will, if utilized, help us recognize our milieu as divine. . . . As Saint Francis knew long ago, the New Creation makes sisters and brothers out of all the birds, the beasts, the fish, the sun, the moon, the stars, and all of humankind."[12] In other words, God is everything and in everything . . . all animals and creation.

During the time of her early career, evangelicals passionately debated the traditional understanding of equality in light of evolving discussions from the civil rights and women's movements collectively. Two official positions, known as the complementarian and the egalitarian views, eventually developed. Both of these views attempted to address pressing social concerns related to equality. Mollenkott relentlessly raised the question of the meaning and social implications of equality in a just and loving society. The extent to which she applied this reasoning is interesting, consistently pushing the boundaries of traditional Christian theology.

Mollenkott's feminism influenced her theological development greatly changing her perceptions of equality and language usage. The New Humanity Mollenkott wanted to establish had broader interpretations of gender than traditional evangelicalism at the time of her writing. More research needs to focus on the specific progression of individual hermeneutical and theological methodology related to her feminism, such as various interpretations of biblical passages related to male/female ontology.

New Hermeneutical Methodology

Mollenkott's loyalty to feminism grew in relation to her use of newer hermeneutical methods. In *Women, Men, & the Bible*, she argued for the idea of mutual submission based on her understanding of progressive revelation. She believed that the Apostle Paul's patriarchal culture required him to imply hierarchical relationships that are no longer valid in twentieth century culture. Therefore, these ideas were to be rejected in a concerned contemporary faith.[13] Integral to these developing ideas was the use of newer interpretive methods which rendered alternatives to traditional opinion on key biblical texts. For example, Mollenkott, in her analysis of Genesis 19 and Romans 1, questioned the traditional interpretations of these passages.[14] In her later writings, she also acknowledged increasing influence from sources outside the Bible for her growing theological convictions.[15] Her openness to include these sources began with her changing interpretive methodology.

AUTHORITY AND PERSONAL WHOLENESS

In her book describing her process "out from fundamentalism," Mollenkott candidly stated that her pursuit for wholeness drove her acceptance of the new hermeneutic.[16] She wrote that she switched to her more progressive interpretive principles because she was "desperate for authenticity, for the healing of my self esteem, and for the use of my gifts."[17] Her journey through fundamentalism caused her to question her identity. She wrote of struggling with feeling guilt and frustration because of the teaching that man was totally depraved. She recounted the time when she finally moved past this biblical principle:

> Inasmuch as I still sometimes revert to the judgmentalism and divisiveness of a human ego that is on its own in a hostile world, the process continues. But

there was for me one distinct 'holy instant' when my basic perception of myself flipped into a different mode. Prior to that "holy instant," I had inched my way from believing myself totally depraved (although redeemed by God's grace) to believing myself a basically decent human being who was having some lovely spiritual experiences. But one day while I was meditating, I experienced a reality that was even better than that: like my Elder Brother, Jesus, I am a sinless Self traveling through eternity and temporarily having human experiences in a body known as Virginia Ramey Mollenkott.[18]

She recalled seeking guidance from the Bible, tarot cards, the *I Ching*, the psychological study *A Course in Miracles*, and dream interpretation.[19]

Mollenkott's hermeneutical technique itself must first be scrutinized. By placing her pursuit of wholeness at the center of her hermeneutics, Mollenkott employed the strategy of approaching the Scripture through a *crux interpretum*.[20] This approach is described by Mary Kassian, noted critic of feminist hermeneutics, as approaching the Bible with a lens of the woman's freedom as the purpose for reading. Mollenkott demonstrated this practice in her admission of allowing her personal wholeness to drive her study of the Bible. While it is true that everyone comes to the text with personal presuppositions, the challenge of interpretation is not reading in order to prove one's views or to achieve social agendas. The complexity of this issue is well acknowledged by biblical scholars. Whether one can ever rid oneself of the influence of personal needs is of much discussion among hermeneutical researchers. Mollenkott's early acceptance of newer hermeneutics placed her directly in the middle of this controversy which would only grow over the following three decades.

The emphasis that Mollenkott gave to the pursuit of wholeness is of concern in an evangelical response because it questions the role of the Bible in the Believer's life. Mollenkott relied on her understanding that God existed and revealed Himself in order to heal humanity and the entire creation of their pains and personal wounds. While it is true that redemption is at the heart of God's activity in history from an evangelical lens, His purpose for revealing Himself is according to His nature and His own purposes, which include but are not limited to humanity's need alone. When Mollenkott wrote that she primarily allowed her personal needs to direct her spiritual path, she revealed a change from traditional evangelical hermeneutics.

According to the traditional evangelical view, the faithful student of the Bible studies in order to show themselves approved (2 Tim 3). There is a humility needed in biblical interpretation which confesses the realization that God is God, and His children read and study His word because it is truth. Healing and redemption are the by products of knowing God, however, seeking the benefits only in this search questions the very nature of the truth that sets men free. Mollenkott diverged in her hermeneutical practices, therefore, altering her conclusions related to interpretation.

Mollenkott, however, placed the personal search for wholeness in the middle of her hermeneutical paradigm; omitting the biblical teaching that addresses such problems outside her feminist framework. She admitted to reading the text from "low and outside," or from the perspective that her personal issues transfer onto the way that she reads the Bible.[21] She also encouraged her readers to become conscious of practicing similar interpretive principles. The question for Mollenkott from evangelical theology, then, is why place such emphasis on this one pursuit? Certainly, sin caused much pain and turmoil. However, the Bible addresses the problem of pain in human life. Paul, in 2 Corinthians 5:18–19 states:

> Now all things are of God, who has reconciled us to Himself through Jesus Christ, and has given us the ministry of reconciliation, that is God was in Christ reconciling the world to Himself, not imputing their trespasses to them, and has committed to us the word of reconciliation.

Why, then, does Mollenkott, who professed to be an evangelical Christian, not equally consider and acknowledge this teaching of Scripture? In Romans 5:7 the Apostle Paul says, "For scarcely for a righteous man will one die; yet perhaps for a good man someone would even dare to die. But God demonstrates His own love toward us, in that while we were still sinners, Christ died for us." The Bible states that to be free from sin and to be whole one must have a salvific relationship with Jesus Christ.[22] However, Mollenkott did not address these Bible passages with similar attention as her theology evolved. She dealt primarily with those passages that were salient to her feminist principles and new hermeneutical methodology. Yet the question remains for Mollenkott: Why does this pursuit for wholeness take on such a prominent role within her interpretive style? She did not attempt to apply the teaching of Scripture that addresses such needs at all, or reconcile the tension they created with the traditional evangelical understanding.

Her foundational argument for the pursuit of personal and societal wholeness as the central interpretive question in hermeneutical methodology is inconsistent for several reasons. First, from where does Mollenkott acquire her definition of personal and societal wholeness? She wrote:

> Western society is currently involved in a crisis of gender definition. Throughout all the centuries of heteropatriarchy, the concept of two opposite sexes has served as a boundary to hold in place the established patterns of power. The binary gender construct has dictated that real males must be naturally drawn to those attitudes, behaviors, and roles any given society considers "masculine,"

including sexual attraction to females only. And real females must be naturally drawn to those attitudes, behaviors, and roles any given society considers "feminine," including sexual attraction to males only.[23]

To accept Mollenkott's thought system is to see that she continually argued against the evangelical paradigm of wholeness as expressed in heterosexuality.

She wrote that there were at least three things wrong with the binary gender concept of traditional orthodoxy. She explained:

> In the first place, the binary gender construct ignores or contradicts factual reality. . . . In the second place, societies vary radically in their understandings of what constitutes "masculinity" and "femininity" (that is, in their gender roles). . . . In the third place, the social construction of gender has not been even-handed about the assignment of roles and rewards.[24]

Therefore, she believed that this expression of reality should be rejected because it inhibited all people who did not fit into this paradigm, thus keeping them from experiencing wholeness and health. However, Mollenkott did not address the question of why one should remain concerned about the traditional evangelical perception of sexuality and gender while simultaneously rejecting the older hermeneutical practices. The question is why did she continue to allow old patriarchal stereotypes to impede on her happiness and pursuit for wholeness?

AUTHORITY AND WORLD RELIGIONS

Mollenkott, throughout her public career, acknowledged her belief in the authority of the Bible. She stated that she believed that reading it with respect for its teachings was important to her throughout her journey.[25] She also believed that her personal experience of wholeness should inform the way that she read the Bible. The issue arises: if Mollenkott believed in the authority of the Scripture, then how did she also believe in the authoritative nature of world religions? Authority and its implications were debated early on in the use of newer hermeneutics. Mollenkott mirrored this debate in her acceptance of authoritative sources outside Scripture from other religions.

While Mollenkott believed that the Bible must be the source for personal beliefs, she also believed that God was the one Source of all truth.[26] Therefore, influence from outside religions was acceptable to Mollenkott. She openly discussed the influence that her experience in dialogue with women of other faiths had on her own journey. However, the question is how she can hold these two beliefs at the same time. She believed the source of the problem was in

Christianity itself. She wrote, "However, the problem stems not from monotheism itself, but from the arrogant notion that any person or any religious group knows all there is to know about the one God."[27] In this sense, Mollenkott's new hermeneutics were central to the issue. Authorship and interpretation are key ideas related to understanding original meanings of texts and their application. Her changing ideas of authority and interpretation are related.

The central issue: The authority of the Bible. Mollenkott stated she approached all questions of life, sexuality, and gender from the standpoint of the biblical teaching.[28] Yet she allowed sources from outside the Bible to influence her beliefs, her life, and her interpretive practices that traditionally were considered to contradict biblical teachings on these subjects. The question, from an evangelical perspective, is why? If Mollenkott did respect the Bible and appreciate its teachings as she said she did, why did she allow so many outside authoritative influences in her hermeneutics?

Ultimately of question in Mollenkott's hermeneutics is her belief in the authority of the Bible. While she stated she believed and adhered to basic interpretive principles which respected biblical authority, increasing influence from sources outside Christianity and its sacred text contradict this statement. For instance, in *Women, Men, & the Bible*, Mollenkott stated that one could not assume the biblical support for the headship/submission marriage model because it was based in outdated patriarchal teachings, to do this would be to absolutize culture, or apply ancient principles to modern life. [29] By assuming that Paul dealt with patriarchal principles because that was the spirit of the age he lived in was to question the ability and intentions of God in the inspiration of the text. This belief also created doubt in the mind and heart of the believer because at what point can the text be trusted? When can one be sure that the text is no longer applicable to ancient cultural traditions only? And who directs this endeavor?

Mollenkott recognized this problem in her approach. She wrote:

> The first problem focuses on biblical evidence in general: Can the Bible be used to prove just anything the arguer wants to prove? The second problem is closely related to the first: if we concede that the Bible does teach male-female equality in the home and in the church, then we are admitting that it has been misinterpreted for centuries. Where will the process of reinterpreting the Bible stop, once we make such an admission? Will we be forced into total relativism? Will we lose all sense of absolutes? Will we, by granting male-female equality, in effect be destroying the authority of the Bible over our lives?[30]

She recognized the unconventional nature of the hermeneutical principles she was suggesting, yet she encouraged them nonetheless. In fact, she exhorted her readers that to question the biblical text in this way was honorable and courageous. To Mollenkott, this took a bravery of mind to interact with the text in this way.[31] Yet, in my perspective, what it did was leave room for the authoritative influence of outside sources without addressing this tension carefully with regard to its complexities.

The real question to be addressed in this aspect of critique of Mollenkott's hermeneutics is the difference between what she said she believed and what she practiced. Repeatedly, Mollenkott declared that she upheld biblical authority and that she felt called of God to remain biblical; however, she did not adhere to the basic principles and practices of an evangelical Christian. Mollenkott believed that by embracing new interpretive methods she was enabling greater intellectual dialogue. However, the question needs to be asked: is the extent to which Mollenkott went outside the influence and teaching of Scripture necessary? She did not just attempt to consider and reconcile anthropological sources or studies in psychology. Arguably, she viewed new research in these areas, specific to gender, with higher regard than Scripture; and where more traditional renderings of Scripture contradicted them often she disregarded those interpretations.

One cannot hold to a belief and then exhibit behavior opposite of those beliefs. She claimed that she held to a high view of Scripture, but her hermeneutical practices were not consistent with these beliefs. By addressing the cultural influence upon the biblical authors, adhering to new and innovative meanings for biblical words, and her belief in progressive revelation Mollenkott demonstrated her divergent opinion of biblical authority. As an early thinker and responder to gender issues in culture, Mollenkott certainly is to be commended for attempting to address these issues. It should also be acknowledged that she was courageous in her interaction with women from other faith traditions. However, it seems that Mollenkott's interpretive methods too easily gave weight and validation to other sources of truth. Therefore, her hermeneutics were not only newer, they were also developing beyond the evangelical community of faith.

Early on she admitted realizing the course in which her hermeneutics could take her. She believed that it was worth the risk, though, in the pursuit of wholeness and the liberation of historically oppressed people within evangelicalism and broader society. Increasingly, however, Mollenkott's practices revealed her weakening view of the authority of Scripture, and her hermeneutics grew more radical over time. However, the two questions that she needed to reconcile with her evangelical interpretive methods were the validity of her pursuit for wholeness and the central issue of the authority of the Bible.

New Understanding of Soteriology

Mollenkott was very open about the fact that her changing understanding of salvation came from her encounters with women outside the Christian faith.[32]

These encounters led her to question the validity of her beliefs that seemed rigid and strict in her expanding theology. As Mollenkott's concept of sin and depravity changed from her Plymouth Brethren faith, she realized that maybe other people were not wrong in other faith systems, either. Therefore, salvation became a much broader concept for Mollenkott. Her beliefs in feminism first moved her understanding to a social freedom as salvation, and then later to a salvific morality.[33] This morality, however, is governed by the coming of the New Humanity in which no predetermined gender role distinctions exist. Mollenkott's loyalty to her new soteriology is driven by her desire for the New Humanity in which diversity is respected and accepted. Soteriology in this sense means personal wholeness through acceptance. Therefore, the new egalitarian humanity is established as each person is saved through their journey toward personal wholeness and recognition of God's Spirit within them; hence, the role of her new soteriological beliefs in her feminist theology.

Mollenkott's view of salvation also progressed outside the bounds of orthodox Christianity throughout her public years of ministry. What began as an acceptance of the traditional view of salvation through Christ alone eventually changed altogether. Although she claimed she believed this soteriological position, she also ascribed to an ever broadening view of salvation. She wrote:

> The traditional Christian interpretation of the righteous servant tends to spotlight Jesus of Nazareth as a one-time only phenomenon, someone out of the past at whose feet we may happily and lazily grovel, someone who will rescue us single-handedly and who thus relieves us of our contemporary responsibility to struggle to bring forth justice in the world. At the same time, the traditional Christian interpretation condemns to hell all those who do not understand the righteous servant to refer exclusively to Jesus the Messiah; instead of encouraging us to do justice and love mercy, this interpretation supports anti-Semitism, Christian triumphalism, and human divisiveness in general.[34]

Mollenkott's religious beliefs, as previously stated, became increasingly inclusive. She cherished her work with women from other faiths and credited this time of her life to opening her understanding of spirituality.[35] According to Mollenkott, the just and loving society is one in which acceptance and toleration of personal beliefs and wholeness is championed.[36] Each person is encouraged to find their own freedom through personal authenticity, accepting the choices of others to validate their religious inclinations. This concept, the New Creation, a just and loving society, is salvation itself.[37] However, Mollenkott concurrently argued for an acceptance of the traditional view of salvation in Christ along with her soteriological beliefs in the New Creation. She did this by stating that she herself accepted the old understanding of salvation through Christ alone, while also appreciating the teachings of other religions.[38] By accepting these two ideas at the same time, she believed that she was exhibiting a more generous spirit for all humanity to experience salvation.

Her acceptance of the two views was necessary because of the need to reconcile the patriarchal teaching with the new, inclusive teaching for society. In *Godding* she wrote:

> Traditionally, sin has been defined as selfish pride, a tendency to regard oneself as the ultimate reality, a tendency to use other people as though they were only objects created to meet one's own needs as subject. This seems a very accurate definition of sin when applied to those who are either financially or physically stronger and thus normative over others. But when it is preached by a dominant group to subordinate groups, it becomes an ugly distortion of reality.[39]

While she rejected the traditional view of salvation because she believed it perpetuated patriarchy, she still believed that it had validity in its own right. Mollenkott never argued to reject other faiths absolutely, she wanted to include all of them as legitimate belief systems. In this acceptance and tolerance of all beliefs, therefore, a natural order of the New Creation would be established.

The challenge in this line of reasoning, however, exists in the fact that she did not acknowledge the contradiction of these two views. A central teaching of the exclusive salvific claims of Christ necessitates the rejection of salvific claims of other world religions. If a belief system does not profess that the only way to salvation is through Jesus Christ, it is not cohesive with orthodox Christianity. However, in Mollenkott's just and loving New Humanity all forms of religious expression are accepted, including various ways to salvation. Therefore, from the evangelical standpoint, her view of salvation must be questioned in at least two points: first, from her feminist definition of salvation and second, from her universalism.

Mollenkott's Feminist Soteriology

As Mollenkott encountered feminism, she became increasingly enamored with the idea of social freedom for women and all oppressed people. In feminist theology as influenced by liberation theology, social freedom is salvation.[40] Mollenkott demonstrated that she knew the difference between the exclusive claims of Christ and the feminist definitions of sin, salvation, and redemption. However, she repeatedly revealed a discrepancy between what she knew and where she allowed herself to be influenced. Mollenkott stated in her chapter in *Women of Faith in Dialogue* that she viewed the Gospel as the Chief Radicalizer of all oppressed people, including women and gender variant people.[41] She redefined the traditional understandings of sin and salvation based on her acceptance of feminist and liberation theology.

Ultimately, Mollenkott redefined salvation to mean social freedom. She believed that the Christian way of relating was through mutual submission in relationships between the sexes. However, inherent in her argument is a change of focus from salvation through Christ to salvation through social status. She explained:

> It is my assumption that if we are interested in understanding the Christian way of relating to others, the Bible must be our central source, and the teachings and behavior of Jesus must provide our major standard of judgment. Jesus said very little about relationships between men and women, and, as far as we know, he did not marry. But he did teach some important basic principles about how human beings ought to relate to one another. And he was very clear about the qualities which make a person truly great, authoritative, and important in the eyes of God. By studying Jesus' principles and observing his behavior against the background of first-century society, we can achieve a clear concept of the Christian way of relating.[42]

However, Mollenkott omitted discussion of Jesus' teaching on salvation. In Mark 8:36 Jesus asked, "For what will it profit a man if he gains the whole world, and yet loses his soul?" Jesus, in this passage, was urging his disciple to be concerned about eternal issues of the heart and soul, not just with political status and social position. However, Mollenkott addressed Jesus' ideas based on her question of the way that men and women ought to relate to one another.

Mollenkott's Universalist Soteriology

Early theological movement outside of orthodox Christianity was evident in Mollenkott's thinking. In *Women, Men, & the Bible* she advocated panentheism:

> Many Christians have made a serious error by picturing God too exclusively in transcendent terms, as if God were completely removed from humanity and the natural world. We have feared pantheism, which involves the denial of God's personhood by equating God with the forces and laws of the universe. Pantheists assume that God is totally immanent, completely contained within that which is created and therefore limited by it. Because we have shied away from pantheism, we have gone to the opposite extreme and spoken as if God were completely transcendent, completely above and beyond and outside of the created universe (including ourselves).[43]

By arguing that Christians feared moving into pantheism, Mollenkott opened her reasoning to allow for the acceptance of believing that God is inside man, and therefore man is a manifestation of god. She explained it this way, "I am a manifestation of God. God Herself! God Himself! God Itself! Above all. Through all. And in us all."[44] She believed that God was "becoming God's self through the process of my living."[45] Mollenkott saw no contradiction between this type of belief and the Bible. The question occurs, however, in this evaluation of her soteriological beliefs: If Mollenkott truly believed that God is becoming God's Self through individual development and growth, then why not admit this break with traditional views of salvation? Why not argue for salvation alone through the inner process of personal wholeness without even bothering with traditional Christianity? Mollenkott obviously moved farther and farther away from the central teachings of these beliefs, so did she not embrace her movement fully? To accept the ideological spirit of her arguments is to accept a broader inclusivism of ideas and religion. Why, then, did Mollenkott not acknowledge this tension in her growing theology?

Over time, Mollenkott's feminist leanings and activities exposed her to universalism. Personal encounters with feminists from all faith backgrounds caused her to question many of her basic religious beliefs. Her understanding of salvation was no different. She credited her work on the "Women of Faith in Dialogue" project with particularly challenging her assumptions regarding salvation.[46] In the book these women published together, Mollenkott's chapter dealt with the need for more interreligious dialogue from evangelicals. Her conclusions are considered here.

Mollenkott based the need for dialogue of this sort on her idea of universal salvation. Mollenkott's argument for interreligious dialogue was based on her belief that in the end all men and women would be saved.[47] She believed that the earnest and brave attempt to "serve truth and justice for the best of one's understanding" would lead to salvation.[48] Therefore, she urged evangelicals to participate in ecumenical dialogue.

As Mollenkott dialogued with women from other faiths, her compassion caused her to question the claims of Christ for salvation. She moved toward accepting all forms of religious expression as valid for salvation through earnest belief and practice. However, Mollenkott's understanding of these basic theological truths must be scrutinized.

The Exclusivity of Christ

Her changing views on salvation centers question on Mollenkott's position on the exclusive salvific claims of Christ. She did not deal with Jesus' statements such as, "I am the Resurrection and the Life" in John 11:25 or "I am the Bread of Life" in John 6:35. She only exhorted her readers to participate in dialogue and accept other people based on respect for the individual's pursuit of wholeness. After all, as each person found the god within, they were experiencing a little bit of the salvation of the entire universe.[49] She wrote:

> But we err whenever we unconsciously assume that the terms of one religion exclude from the experience being described all people who would not use the same terminology. The experience of godding, which is a spiritual matter of the attitudes that are expressed in human relationships, is open to people of every religion. Across the face of the earth are people of various religions who would use different terms for those who love their neighbors as they love themselves and whose faith is alive because it leads to practical and structural acts of mercy.[50]

Ultimately, Mollenkott moved not only to reject the exclusive claims of Christ, but also to accept the belief that individual humans are manifestations of God's Self. This belief rejects the clear truth claims of Christ for salvation in the Bible. Evangelical theologians traditionally believe that He did not suffer and die to offer one of many opportunities for salvation. He did so because it was the only way to satisfy the wrath of God (Isa 53). Mollenkott allowed her personal experiences and desire for wholeness and healing to motivate her search for answers outside of redemption through Christ alone. Overall, Mollenkott moved consistently outside the boundaries of evangelical theology. In regard to the doctrine of salvation, however, her movement was most visible. Mollenkott's feminist presuppositions and personal encounters in ecumenical dialogue contributed to her evolving understanding of the doctrine of salvation.

Cultural Issues

At the heart of all that Mollenkott wrote and did was her desire to be culturally relevant and active.[51] She believed that to be a good Christian was to be socially aware and concerned for the oppressed in society. The more Mollenkott became concerned for the welfare and wholeness of others, homosexual people and women in particular, the more she opened her positions to validate personal experiences.[52]

She was keenly aware of the painful realities women and homosexual people encountered in secular and Christian patriarchal culture, and she was committed to alleviating their pain. However, Mollenkott increasingly emphasized this need to alleviate suffering over the traditional understanding of biblical authority. Nonetheless, the role of cultural issues in her theology underscores her development in each of the other themes.

HOMOSEXUALITY: CAN YOU ACCEPT
THE SINNER AND NOT THE SIN?

Mollenkott argued that evangelical Christians must not only accept the sinner, but also reject the traditional belief that all forms of homosexuality were sin. By asking the evangelical community to think about homosexuality in terms of relationships that are caring, sincere, and responsible rather than all sinful, Mollenkott created new categories for evaluating sexual preferences and practices in her growing theology. She redefined the biblical position to exclude the practice of homosexuality from being considered a sin. She reinterpreted Genesis 19 and Romans 1 to accommodate this belief for the purposes of being culturally sensitive.

In the case of Genesis 19, Mollenkott concluded that the sin of the men of Sodom and Gomorrah was not that they wanted to have sex with the other men, but that they wanted to rape them.[53] Mollenkott believed that the men were probably heterosexual and only wanted to humiliate the strangers, thus their real sin was revealed.[54] Furthermore, she also believed that the men were found guilty of being inhospitable to the strangers, therefore their judgment was as recorded in Genesis.

In the case of Romans 1, Mollenkott emphasized that the text primarily focused on the "unnatural" aspects of the natural relations of men between men and women between women. In other words, Mollenkott believed that Paul, in this instruction, was prohibiting lust in any human sexual relationships, not just homosexual ones. She stated:

> The key thoughts seem to be lust, "unnaturalness," and, in verse 28, a desire to avoid acknowledgement of God. But although the censure fits the idolatrous people with whom Paul was concerned here, it does not fit the case of a sincere homosexual Christian. Such a person loves Jesus Christ and wants above all to acknowledge God in all of life, yet for some unknown reason feels drawn to someone of the same sex—not because of lust, but because of sincere, heartfelt love. Is it fair to describe that person as lustful or desirous of forgetting God's existence?[55]

Mollenkott was convinced that the true question of biblical support for homosexuality was whether the relationship was one of love or not. She further supported this idea with her interpretation of the Levitical passages that dealt with sexuality.

Mollenkott believed that:

> What we need to keep in mind, however, is that the warnings and condemnations in these various passages are centered around the *idolatrous practices* of

the fertility religions, not whether the ceremonial sexual activity involved men with men or men with women. The people who loved and served the God of Israel were strictly forbidden to have anything to do with idolatry and commanded never to serve, nor to let their children serve, as temple prostitutes (Deut 23:17–18).[56]

Convinced that the purpose of these biblical teachings was to prohibit idolatrous sex acts committed outside of any loving relationships, including homosexual ones, she consistently challenged the traditional interpretations of these passages. Therefore, Mollenkott argued that homosexuality was acceptable in the Bible because it was never addressed in the context of loving commitment. Her newer position accepted both homosexual people and homosexuality, rejecting the belief that all non-heterosexual sexual practices were sinful.

Mollenkott accurately pointed out that the church needed to do a better job of ministering to homosexual people and questions of gender in general. She was correct to assert that, "The matter of sexual orientation is, in fact, far more complex than many Christians realize. It is simplistic to presume that when homosexuals (erotically attracted to the same sex) become Christians, they automatically become heterosexuals (erotically attracted to the opposite sex)."[57] Issues of gender identity and sexuality absolutely strike at the core of human personhood. Therefore, it is clear that ministry in the twenty-first century must address all aspects of gender concerns and topics.

Mollenkott asked the question of whether or not the homosexual is a neighbor. Clearly, the answer is yes. Like the Good Samaritan in the parable of Jesus, however, the responsible task is to acknowledge and address the wounds of the neighbor, rather than simply acknowledging their existence. She based her argument for acceptance of homosexuals because of her concept of compassion. Mollenkott believed that true compassion meant acceptance and affirmation. However, this understanding of compassion should be analyzed.

It would seem that her idea, applied to the Good Samaritan, would mean that the Good Samaritan only saw the sin and pain of the wounded man on the road without taking action to help him. The first religious authorities passed by the hurting person, but did not actually help him. The Samaritan passed by the hurting person, stopped to acknowledge his wounds, and helped him begin the healing process. Should not a ministry to all people, heterosexual and homosexual, be at least this merciful, attempting to address and acknowledge the pain and struggle of sin in each person's life? It would seem that this type of compassion is the form that the Bible, in this parable of the Good Samaritan, actually supports rather than the notion of acceptance and affirmation only.

The Transgender Society

In her last two books, Mollenkott re-envisioned the church and society to be places where "everybody would have their own unique sexuality, falling in love with another person because of their emotional response to the person's entire being, not the person's genitals."[58] She believed that the fullness of salvation meant a society free of gender judgmentalism. Mollenkott considered a place where "people would be considered unisexual in that they could choose to identify themselves and their lover anywhere within the whole spectrum of sexual continuity."[59] She wanted intersexual children to be able to choose their own sex and to be categorized as neither male nor female in this society until they were old enough to recognize who they were. Mollenkott believed that gender freedom to be authentic would symbolize an ideological shift and a movement towards the establishment of the New Humanity.[60]

These ideas are based in her belief that human sexuality is more complex than merely being male and female. She argued that omnigender society must be embraced in order to create a place for the full sexual and gender expression of all persons. She believed that such an idea had to be accepted because otherwise, it was unfair for the Church to admit heterosexual people to express their sexuality inside marriage, while leaving all homosexual, bisexual, lesbian, and transgender people without companionship or expression.

However, Mollenkott ignored the biblical teaching that heterosexuality in itself is not license for sexual expression. God intended the covenant of marriage to be between a man and a woman to be one emotionally, spiritually, and sexually. Though Mollenkott does discuss this aspect of heterosexual marriage in *Women, Men, and the Bible,* how this reality works out in relationships as she grew in her beliefs is omitted in her later writings. Therefore, she argued that in order to be fair to everyone, all types of sexual and gender expression should be validated as long as they are genuinely loving.

When Mollenkott argued for the right and the will of each person to define their own gender identity, she was being consistent with the feminist presupposition to authoritatively create and identify oneself.[61] Understanding and wrestling with the doctrine of creation, and subsequently the doctrine of humanity is at the heart of Mollenkott's theological development. Traditionally, Christianity taught that God, as the Creator, chose to create men and women. To argue, as Mollenkott did, that the church must accept and embrace sexual ambiguity is to question the traditional understanding of the intentions of God in human sexuality. There is a clear correlation with the relationship of the man and woman and the relationships within the Trinity, both 1 Corinthians 11:2–12 and Ephesians 5:22–33 support this fact.

The core issue of how to address pain and suffering, while also interacting with the biblical passages relevant to human autonomy is a central issue in the development of Mollenkott's beliefs. Because she was personally aware of the struggle to accept herself when she did not fit in socially with mainstream evangelical culture, she argued for an omnigender society which would embrace all forms of authentic individual expression. The challenge in her development comes, however, in the use of her hermeneutical method to arrive at these new ideas and wrestling with the doctrine of creation and humanity thoroughly in her progression. Accepting the differences of others is important in any culture, but Mollenkott went further than to accept them, and to affirm and condone them as the central ingredient for cultural relevance. This aspect of her development is at odds with evangelical theology, and needs to be addressed more fully.

Inclusive Language

Throughout Mollenkott's books she advocated the usage of inclusive language. She believed that it would aid the church in several ways. First, it would help women overcome the oppression they had suffered under patriarchy.[62] Second, it would give all people a better understanding of God's Spirit as both masculine and feminine, or neither masculine or feminine. The *Divine Feminine* was devoted solely to the development of this concept. She argued that advancing the use of female God language would be a powerful apologetic for the church in the twentieth century.[63] Mollenkott feared many people had already left Christianity because of its gender exclusive language.[64] As Mollenkott's vision for the omnigender society grew, she believed inclusive language would be instrumental in ushering in the New Humanity.[65] Overall, Mollenkott's commitment to the use of inclusive language permeated her theological development because of her desire to remain culturally aware.

Correct in her assertion that language represents and influences the hearts and minds of people, Mollenkott believed that language had been harmful to women. However, could language itself damage people? Or was it was the hearts of people who misunderstood the nature and intentions of God in the male/female design for relationships? Orthodox evangelical theology held that God instituted the imagery and symbolism of language as expressed in the Created Order. If injustices occurred in society toward women and children it was not the fault of the language itself which represented the intentions of this pattern, but the people. The answer for these injustices is more complex than language usage alone. Addressing the realities and complexities of humanity is the task of all relevant ministry. Thinking clearly and humbly about the possibilities of each person, society, and culture because of sin is the heart of inequality and struggle for power. Mollenkott believed that the way to heal these injustices was to change language. This process would eventually change the hearts of people. However, if the hearts of people were actually the issue, then why not spend time addressing adequately and fully this reality? If there is an issue with language usage, then certainly address it; the question remains how language usage alone is such a vital element in changing people thoroughly. To be relevant culturally is to be sensitive to the role of language, but this is only one factor of awareness in ministry. Addressing others aspects, particularly if the goal is to change the culture itself, as Mollenkott wanted to do in the New Humanity, must have more attention to detail and appreciation for the complexities of life.

Mollenkott began her public career with a concern for the social issues of her day. Her compassion for people outside the mainstream of culture was admirable. She brought a clear call to the renewal in understanding the pain and suffering of people. However, her ideas on the quality of compassion and mercy were very different from evangelical perspectives at the time of her writing. Acknowledging the cultural realities of her time is to be commended, however, the ways in which she sought to address those issues were challenging to her theology and its practical application. It is important to understand and acknowledge her perceptions, however, her methodology is open to question. However, as one of the first to address these cultural concerns, she is to be acknowledged as the pioneer voice in culturally relevant ministry as it pertains to gender.

RESEARCH IMPLICATIONS AND APPLICATIONS OF MOLLENKOTT'S THEOLOGY

Virginia Ramey Mollenkott lived through much personal and cultural change. Acknowledging difficulties of her childhood beliefs with growing educational acumen challenged her opinions greatly. She was one of the first evangelical women to attempt the integration of feminism into her Christianity. As has been stated in this study, Mollenkott's theology progressed beyond the bounds of evangelical Christian orthodoxy throughout the span of her career. In this section, research implications and applications from this critical analysis of her theology are offered. The theological themes and critique of her movement are both under consideration for specific areas within the evangelical community. Research implications are offered first.

Research Implications

From this study several implications begin to emerge from the life and thought of Virginia Ramey Mollenkott. Clearly, she was an advocate in the church for the acceptance of feminist theology within evangelicalism. In fact, she was one of the first evangelicals to embrace these teachings.[66] She did so from the earnest belief that the gospel was the Great Liberator of women, and that the concepts of feminism were the best avenue to achieve this freedom.[67] However, Mollenkott's evangelical theology changed throughout the years. What began as a desire to see men and women treated equally in society and the church led to an ever-broadening view of sin, salvation, and God.

Mollenkott's journey is not unlike other women who embraced feminism during the latter twentieth century. However, her particular story is unique because she began from a Plymouth Brethren, evangelical background. Therefore, her movement coincided with the development of the egalitarian position. Though the formal establishment of this position took place when some egalitarian leaders parted with the Evangelical Women's Caucus and Mollenkott in particular, streams of her thought are still evident in their beliefs. While advocates of this view do not affirm the acceptance of homosexuality in the church, they do accept some of the hermeneutics Mollenkott used to reach her positions.[68]

SUGGESTIONS FOR FURTHER RESEARCH

From the research presented in this book, several possible other studies emerge. First, a continuing and robust conversation surrounding the implications of human dignity and human rights is necessary in the evangelical world. Understanding the cultural studies of anthropologists and sociologists in light of biblical truth is long overdue within evangelicalism. The divisive nature of the gender debate has delayed progress in discussions related to human rights and equality issues. The great contradictions in statistics in the evangelical community about divorce rates and cohabiting couples alone merit some critical discourse on the discussions centered on the "traditional family" and its related "values" discussion. However, whether one agrees or disagrees with Virginia Mollenkott, certainly her contribution is the consistent voice to consider those "low and outside." This discussion has not been sufficiently acknowledged to this point within evangelicalism, and it is time for it to be seriously addressed.

Second, a study could be done on another significant figure in the theological gender debate. One such example could be Catherine Kroeger. She would be interesting because she was a contemporary with Mollenkott, however, when the issue of homosexuality became the dividing factor within religious feminism, Kroeger rejected affirming homosexuality as an acceptable biblical possibility.

Another possible research topic would be a comparative study of the lives of several complementarians and egalitarians. In this type of work, the researcher could compare and contrast several theological emphases, then observe how they have been applied in the lives of the selected scholars from each view. This type of work would be interesting to see how the theological works affected the lives of these people.

Significant work is yet to be done addressing the continued influence and voice evangelicals have in general regarding issues related to gender in broader culture. How does a Christian think through a biblical response to cultural events of the last fifty or sixty years? Are compassionate and comprehensive ministry efforts being made to help laypeople understand the relevance of the gender debate in culture? In what ways are Christians educated to understand what these implications are? All of these questions are relevant to the life and theology of Virginia Mollenkott. Wherever one tends to stand in relation to her ideas, her thought challenges everyone to consider what they believe and what difference this makes in the world around them. Further thought and research needs to be given to clearly and carefully addressing the growing questions of sexuality and gender in culture.

A final suggestion for further research would be to choose one theological theme and trace the development of that theme in the thought of several feminist theologians. In particular, the relationship between universalism and feminism would be interesting. Mollenkott's commitment to feminism eventually allowed her movement into universalism. It would be interesting to trace if this movement was evident in the thought of other feminist theologians.

CONCLUSION

Ultimately, the question of biblical interpretation is central to the evolution of the theology of Virginia Ramey Mollenkott. Although she did address biblical interpretation throughout her writings, in my mind, ultimately she allowed her personal pursuit of wholeness; feminist presuppositions; new hermeneutical methodology; new soteriology; and cultural concerns to dictate the development of her thought. Throughout her personal and faith development, by integrating feminism into her theology caused Mollenkott's beliefs to change over time. This study should challenge and exhort further clarity on the evangelical teachings and ministry implications of issues related to gender.

As a person, Mollenkott experienced much change and turmoil, and this reality influenced her theology. She was also a catalyst for change inside and outside the evangelical community, serving on a board for the National

Council of Churches and speaking at an event for the National Organization for Women. Mollenkott's development is interesting as it is the biography of one person's life at a historically significant moment in American culture. How it affected her theological progression is instructive for those who desire to understand both culture and implications for theology and ministry. While her conclusions might not be accepted by the broader evangelical community, her desire to understand and show compassion to every person was sincere.

As one who does not fully accept all of Mollenkott's feminist theology, there is still much to be learned and appreciated from her challenge to understand the role of equality and social justice. Pursuing rigorous biblical and theological scholarship alongside honest and compassionate ministry is the challenge of Mollenkott for evangelicals who disagree with her. For those who agree, the challenge of ideological honesty and rigor is similar, with variant implications. The degree to which someone can remain a part of a community, yet change and question the mainstream definitions of that community, both for evangelicalism and feminism, is inherent in Mollenkott's theological progression. Both of these questions need further pursuit. For the purposes of a work considering the broad contribution of Virginia Mollenkott, her scholarship and her desire for equality for all people was clear and commendable.

NOTES

1. Virginia R. Mollenkott, *Speech, Silence, Action! The Cycle of Faith* (Nashville: Abingdon, 1980), 22.
2. Mollenkott, *Sensuous Spirituality*, 16.
3. Mollenkott, *Speech, Silence, Action!*, 58.
4. Ibid., 65.
5. Mollenkott, *Adamant and Stone Chips*, 27.
6. Ibid., 27–28.
7. Mollenkott, *Sensuous Spirituality*, 167.
8. Ibid.
9. Mollenkott, *Women, Men, & the Bible*, 39.
10. Mollenkott, *Women, Men, & the Bible*, 72.
11. Ibid.
12. Mollenkott, *The Divine Feminine*, 109.
13. Mollenkott, *Women, Men, & the Bible*, 82.
14. Mollenkott, *Is the Homosexual My Neighbor?*, 57, 72.
15. Mollenkott, *Sensuous Spirituality*, 18.
16. Mollenkott, *Sensuous Spirituality*, 16.
17. Ibid., 68–69.
18. Ibid., 16.

19. Ibid.
20. Kassian, *The Feminist Mistake*, 131.
21. Mollenkott, "A Call to Subversion."
22. See John 14:6.
23. Ibid., 1.
24. Ibid., 3.
25. Mollenkott, *Women, Men, & the Bible*, 1.
26. Mollenkott, *Godding*, 4–5.
27. Ibid., 5.
28. Mollenkott, *Women, Men, & the Bible*, 1.
29. Ibid., 74.
30. Mollenkott, *Women, Men, & the Bible*, 88.
31. Ibid., 90.
32. Ibid.
33. Mollenkott, *Omnigender*, vii.
34. Mollenkott, *Godding*, 7.
35. Mollenkott, *Women of Faith in Dialogue*, 71.
36. Mollenkott, *Godding*, 2.
37. Ibid., 6.
38. Ibid., 7.
39. Ibid., 84.
40. Rosemary R. Ruether, *Liberation Theology: Human Hope Confronts Christian History and American Power* (New York: Paulist Press, 1972), 9.
41. Mollenkott, *Women of Faith in Dialogue*, 63.
42. Mollenkott, *Women, Men, & the Bible*, 1–2.
43. Mollenkott, *Women, Men, & the Bible*, 107–08.
44. Mollenkott, *Godding*, 6.
45. Ibid., 4.
46. Ibid., 62.
47. Ibid., 66.
48. Ibid.
49. Mollenkott, *Godding*, 8.
50. Ibid.
51. Mollenkott, *Speech, Silence, Action!*, 11.
52. Mollenkott, *Godding*, 84.
53. Mollenkott and Scanzoni, *Is the Homosexual My Neighbor?*, 58.
54. Ibid., 59.
55. Ibid., 67.
56. Ibid., 64.
57. Ibid., 4.
58. Mollenkott, *Omnigender*, 167.
59. Ibid.
60. Ibid., 150.
61. Kassian, *The Feminist Mistake*, 89.
62. Mollenkott, *Women, Men, & the Bible*, 39.

63. Mollenkott, *Divine Feminine*, 2.

64. Ibid.

65. Mollenkott, *Omnigender*, 169.

66. Pamela Cochran, *Evangelical Feminism: A History* (New York: New York University Press, 2005), 9.

67. Mollenkott, *Women of Faith in Dialogue*, 63.

68. An example of this agreement in methodology is seen in the hermeneutics Catherine and Richard Kroeger argued for in their treatment of the cultural argument for Eve in the 1 Tim 2:11–15 teaching on women in the church. Because the surrounding Ephesian church probably had cultural problems, the Kroegers argue that the text should not be applied to life today. This reasoning is the same line of thought Mollenkott used in her "de-absolutization" of culture. Catherine C. Kroeger and Richard C. Kroeger, *I Suffer Not a Woman* (Grand Rapids: Baker, 1992), 153–60.

Bibliography

Achtemier, Elizabeth. "Female Language for God: Should the Church Adopt It?" In *The Hermeneutical Quest*. Pickwick, NJ: Allison Park, 1986.

Aleshire, Daniel. "Papers and Presentations" [on-line]. *The Association of Theological Schools* (2003). Accessed 18 November 2005. Available from http://www.ats . edu/leadership_education/Papers2003Aleshire1asp; Internet.

Allen, Prudence. *The Concept of Woman: The Aristotelian Revolution, 750 BC—AD 1250*. Montréal: Eden, 1985.

Anderson, Pamela Sue. *A Feminist Philosophy of Religion: The Rationality and Myths of Religious Belief*. Malden, MA: Blackwell, 1998.

Bailey, Derrick S. *Homosexuality and the Western Christian Tradition*. London: Longman, Green, 1955.

Baker, James R. *Women's Rights in Old Testament Times*. Salt Lake City: Signature, 1992.

Barry, Catherine, and Virginia R. Mollenkott. *Views from the Intersection*. New York: Crossroad, 1984.

Baumgardner, Jennifer, and Amy Richards. *Manifesta: Young Women, Feminism, and the Future*. New York: Farrar, Straus, and Giroux, 2000.

Bell, Alan P., Martin S. Weinberg, Sue Kiefer Hammersmith, and Alfred C. Kinsey Institute for Sex Research. *Sexual Preference, Its Development in Men and Women*. Bloomington: Indiana University Press, 1981.

Belleville, Linda L. *Women Leaders and the Church: 3 Crucial Questions*. Grand Rapids: Baker, 2000.

Berkouwer, G. C., and Jack Bartlett Rogers. *Holy Scripture*. Grand Rapids: W. B. Eerdmans, 1975.

Bilezikian, Gilbert G. *Beyond Sex Roles: A Guide for the Study of Female Roles in the Bible*. Grand Rapids: Baker, 1985.

Boswell, John. *Christianity, Social Tolerance, and Homosexuality: Gay People in Western Europe from the Beginning of the Christian Era to the Fourteenth Century*. Chicago: University of Chicago Press, 1980.

Børresen, Kari Elisabeth, ed. *The Image of God: Gender Models in Judea-Christian Tradition*. Minneapolis: Fortress, 1995.

Brenner, Athalya. *The Feminist Companion to the Bible*. Sheffield, England: Sheffield Academic Press, 1993.

Bronner, Leila Leah. *From Eve to Esther: Rabbinic Reconstructions of Biblical Women*. Gender and the Biblical Tradition. Louisville: Westminster/John Knox, 1994.

Bundesen, Lynne. *The Woman's Guide to the Bible*. New York: Crossroad, 1993.

Butler, Judith. *Gender Trouble: Feminism and the Subversion of Identity Thinking Gender*. New York: Routledge, 1990.

Carmody, Denise Lardner. *Biblical Woman: Contemporary Reflections on Scriptural Texts*. New York: Crossroad, 1988.

Carr, Anne. "Is Christian Feminist Theology Possible?" *Theological Studies* 43, no. 2 (1982): 279–97.

Carson, D. A. *The Inclusive-Language Debate: A Plea for Realism*. Grand Rapids: Baker, 1998.

Christ, Carol P. "The New Feminist Theology: A Review of the Literature." *Religious Studies Review* 3 (1977): 203–12.

Christians for Biblical Equality [on-line]. Accessed 18 March 2005. Available from http://www.cbeinternational.org; Internet.

Clark, Stephen B. *Man and Woman in Christ: An Examination of the Roles of Men and Women in Light of Scripture and the Social Sciences*. Ann Arbor: Servant, 1980.

Cochran, Pamela. *Evangelical Feminism: A History*. New York: New York University Press, 2005.

Cook, Kaye V., and Lance Lee. *Man & Woman: Alone & Together*. Wheaton, IL: Victor, 1992.

Cott, Nancy F. *The Grounding of Modern Feminism*. New Haven, CT: Yale University Press, 1987.

Cottrell, Jack. *Feminism and the Bible: An Introduction to Feminism for Christians*. Joplin, MO: College Press, 1992.

The Council on Biblical Manhood and Womanhood Staff. *The Council on Biblical Manhood and Womanhood* [on-line]. Accessed 18 March 2005. Available from http://www.cbmw.org/about/mission.php; Internet.

Daly, Lois K. *Feminist Theological Ethics: A Reader*. Library of Theological Ethics. Louisville: Westminster/John Knox, 1994.

Daly, Mary. *The Church and the Second Sex*. London: G. Chapman, 1968.

DeBeauvoir, Simone. *The Second Sex*. New York: Random, 1989.

DeBerg, Betty A. *Ungodly Women: Gender and the First Wave of American Fundamentalism*. Minneapolis: Fortress, 1990.

DeMoss, Nancy Leigh. *Biblical Womanhood in the Home*. Wheaton, IL: Crossway, 2002.

Edwards, George R. *Gay/Lesbian Liberation: A Biblical Perspective*. New York: Pilgrim, 1984.

Eggebroten, Anne. "Handing Power." *The Other Side* (December 1986): 20–25.

Erickson, Millard J. *Christian Theology*. 2nd ed. Grand Rapids: Baker, 1998.

Evans, Mary J. *Woman in the Bible: An Overview of All the Crucial Passages on Women's Roles*. Downers Grove, IL: InterVarsity, 1984.

Fausto-Sterling, Anne. *Myths of Gender: Biological Theories about Women and Men*. 2nd ed. New York: Basic, 1992.

Findlen, Barbara. *Listen Up: Voices from the Next Feminist Generation*. New exp. ed. Seattle: Seal, 2001.

Fitzmyer, Joseph A. *Scripture, the Soul of Theology*. New York: Paulist, 1994.

Foh, Susan T. *Women and the Word of God: A Response to Biblical Feminism*. Philadelphia: Presbyterian and Reformed, 1980.

France, R. T. *Women in the Church's Ministry: A Test-Case for Biblical Interpretation*. Grand Rapids: W. B. Eerdmans, 1997.

Franklin, William, and Joseph M. Shaw. *The Case for Christian Humanism*. Grand Rapids: William B. Eerdmans, 1991.

Gallagher, Sally K. *Evangelical Identity and Gendered Family Life*. New Brunswick, CT: Rutgers University Press, 2003

Geis, Sally B., and Donald E. Messer. *Caught in the Crossfire: Helping Christians Debate Homosexuality*. Nashville: Abingdon, 1994.

Gilder, George F. *Sexual Suicide*. New York: Quadrangle, 1973.

Goldberg, Steven. *The Inevitability of Patriarchy*. New York: Morrow, 1973.

Graham, Anne. *Womanhood Revisited: A Fresh Look at Women in Society*. Fern, Great Britain: Christian Focus, 2002.

Granberg-Michaelson, Karin. *We Are Who We Are by the Grace of God* [on-line]. RCA: Journal of Reformed Thought, 2003. Accessed 14 March 2005. Available from http://www.perspectivesjournal.org/2003/08/interview.php/:Internet.

Grenz, Stanley J., and Denise Muir Kjesbo. *Women in the Church: A Biblical Theology of Women in Ministry*. Downers Grove, IL: InterVarsity, 1995.

Groothuis, Rebecca Merrill. *Good News for Women: A Biblical Picture of Gender Equality*. Grand Rapids: Baker, 1997.

Grudem, Wayne A. *Evangelical Feminism & Biblical Truth: An Analysis of More Than One Hundred Disputed Questions*. Sisters, OR: Multnomah, 2004.

Gundry, Patricia. *Neither Slave nor Free: Helping Women Answer the Call to Church Leadership*. San Francisco: Harper & Row, 1987.

———. *Woman, Be Free!* Grand Rapids: Zondervan, 1977.

Hagen, June Steffensen. *Rattling Those Dry Bones: Women Changing the Church*. San Diego: LuraMedia, 1995

Hampson, Margaret Daphne. *Theology and Feminism* Signposts in Theology. Cambridge: B. Blackwell, 1990.

Hardesty, Nancy. "Evangelical Women Face Their Homophobia." *Christian Century*, August 1986, 768.

———. *Inclusive Language in the Church*. Atlanta: J. Knox, 1987.

———. *Women Called to Witness : Evangelical Feminism in the Nineteenth Century*. 2nd ed. Knoxville: University of Tennessee Press, 1999.

Hauke, Manfred. *God or Goddess? Feminist Theology: What Is It? Where Does It Lead?* San Francisco: Ignatius, 1995.

————. *Women in the Priesthood?: A Systematic Analysis in the Light of the Order of Creation and Redemption*. San Francisco: Ignatius, 1988

Hestenes, Roberta, and Lois Curley, eds. *Women and the Ministries of Christ*. Pasadena: Fuller Theological Seminary, 1979.

Heyward, Carter. *Touching Our Strength: The Erotic as Power and the Love of God*. San Francisco: Harper & Row, 1989.

Heyward, Carter, and Ellen C. Davis. *Speaking of Christ: A Lesbian Feminist Voice*. New York: Pilgrim, 1989.

Horner, Sue S. "Becoming All We're Meant to Be: A Social History of the Contemporary Evangelical Feminist Movement, a Case Study of the Evangelical and Ecumenical Women's Caucus." Ph.D. diss., Garrett-Evangelical Theological Seminary, 2000.

————. *How Did EEWC Originate?* Evangelical and Ecumenical Women's Caucus, 2001 [on-line]. Accessed 19 February 2005. Available from http://www.eewc.com/About.html; Internet.

House, H. Wayne. *The Role of Women in Ministry Today*. Grand Rapids: Baker, 1995.

Hove, Richard. *Equality in Christ? Galatians 3:28 and the Gender Dispute*. Wheaton, IL: Crossway, 1999.

Hull, Gretchen Gaebelein. *Equal to Serve: Women and Men in the Church and Home*. Old Tappan, NJ: F. H. Revell, 1987.

Hunt, Susan. *By Design: God's Distinctive Calling for Women*. 2nd ed. Wheaton, IL: Crossway, 1998.

————. *The True Woman: The Beauty and Strength of a Godly Woman*. Wheaton, IL: Crossway, 1997.

Hurley, James B. *Man and Woman in Biblical Perspective*. Grand Rapids: Zondervan, 1981.

Ingersoll, Julie. *Evangelical Christian Women: War Stories in the Gender Battles*. Qualitative Studies in Religion. New York: New York University Press, 2003.

Jewett, Paul King. *Man as Male and Female: A Study in Sexual Relationships from a Theological Point of View*. Grand Rapids: Eerdmans, 1975.

Jewett, Paul King, and Marguerite Shuster. *Who We Are: Our Dignity as Human: A Neo-Evangelical Theology*. Grand Rapids: W. B. Eerdmans, 1996.

Kassian, Mary A. *The Feminist Gospel: The Movement to Unite Feminism with the Church*. Wheaton, IL: Crossway, 1992.

————. *The Feminist Mistake*. Wheaton, IL: Crossway, 2004.

————. *Women, Creation, and the Fall*. Wheaton, IL: Crossway, 1990.

Kau, Ina. "Feminists in the American Evangelical Movement." Master's thesis, Pacific School of Religion, 1977.

Keener, Craig S. *Paul, Women & Wives: Marriage and Women's Ministry in the Letters of Paul*. Peabody, MA: Hendrickson, 1992.

King, Ursula. *Women in the World's Religions, Past and Present*. God, the Contemporary Discussion Series. New York: Paragon, 1987.

Kirschbaum, Charlotte von. *The Question of Woman: The Collected Writings of Charlotte Von Kirschbaum*. Translated by J. Shepherd, ed. E. Jackson. Grand Rapids: W. B. Eerdmans, 1996.

Knight, George W., Wayne A. Grudem, and George W. Knight. *The Role Relationship of Men and Women: New Testament Teaching*. Rev. ed. Chicago: Moody, 1985.

Köstenberger, Andreas J., and David W. Jones. *God, Marriage & Family: Rebuilding the Biblical Foundation*. Wheaton, IL: Crossway, 2004.

Köstenberger, Andreas J., Thomas R. Schreiner, and H. Scott Baldwin. *Women in the Church: A Fresh Analysis of I Timothy 2:9–15*. Grand Rapids: Baker, 1995.

Kridl, Barbara, ed. "The Condition of Education 2001" [on-line]. *National Center for Education Statistics* (June 2001). Accessed 18 November 2005. Available from http://nces.ed.gov/pubs2001/2001072.pdf; Internet.

Kroeger, Richard Clark, and Catherine Clark Kroeger. *I Suffer Not a Woman: Rethinking 1 Timothy 2:11–15 in Light of Ancient Evidence*. Grand Rapids: Baker, 1992.

Lewis, C. S. *That Hideous Strength; a Modern Fairy-Tale for Grownups*. New York: Macmillan, 1968.

———. *The Weight of Glory*. New York: Macmillan, 1965.

Loades, Ann, and Karen Armstrong. *Feminist Theology: A Reader*. Louisville: Westminster/John Knox, 1990.

Malcolm, Kari. "Who Will Be Real? When Will We Be Free?" *Priscilla Papers* 1, no. 1 (1987): 1–2.

Malkmus, Doris. *Lgbtran—Oral History Project* Religious Archives Network [on-line]. Accessed 13 June 2005. Available from http://www.lgbtran.org/Exhibits/Mollenkott/Bio.htm; Internet.

Marsden, George M. *Fundamentalism and American Culture: The Shaping of Twentieth Century Evangelicalism*. New York: Oxford University Press, 1980.

———. *Understanding Fundamentalism and Evangelicalism*. Grand Rapids: W. B. Eerdmans, 1991.

Martin, Francis. *The Feminist Question: Feminist Theology in the Light of Christian Tradition*. Grand Rapids: W. B. Eerdmans, 1994.

McConnell-Celi, Sue. *Twenty-First Century Challenge: Lesbians and Gays in Education, Bridging the Gap*. Red Bank, NJ: Lavender Crystal, 1993.

McNeill, John J. *The Church and the Homosexual*. Updated and exp. ed. Boston: Beacon, 1988.

———. *Taking a Chance on God: Liberating Theology for Gays, Lesbians, and Their Lovers, Families, and Friends*. Boston: Beacon, 1988.

Mickelsen, Alvera. *Women, Authority & the Bible*. Downers Grove, IL: InterVarsity, 1986.

Mollenkott, Virginia R. *Adam among the Television Trees; an Anthology of Verse by Contemporary Christian Poets*. Waco, TX: Word Books, 1971.

———. *Adamant & Stone Chips: A Christian Humanist Approach to Knowledge*. Waco, TX: Word Books, 1968.

———. "The Bible and Inclusive Language." *The Other Side*, no. 11 (1986): 14–19.

———. "Critical Inquiry and Biblical Inerrancy." *Religion and Public Education: The Journal of the National Council on Religion and Public Education* (Winter 1990): 87.

———. *The Divine Feminine: The Biblical Imagery of God as Female*. New York: Crossroad, 1983.

———. "An Evangelical Feminist Confronts the Goddess." *Christian Century* (October 1982): 1043–046.

———. "Evangelicalism: A Feminist Perspective." *Union Seminary Quarterly* 32, no. 2 (1977): 95–103.

———. "Female God-Imagery and Wholistic Social Consciousness." *Studies in Formative Spirituality* (November 1984): 345–54.

———. "Feminism and the Kingdom: From Machismo to Mutuality." *Sojourners* 6 (1977): 28–30.

———. *Godding: Human Responsibility and the Bible.* New York: Crossroad, 1987.

———. *In Search of Balance.* Waco, TX: Word, 1969.

———. *Omnigender: A Trans-Religious Approach.* Cleveland: Pilgrim, 2001.

———. "Reproductive Choice: Basic Justice for Women." *Christian Scholar's Review* 17, no. 3 (1988): 286–93.

———. *Sensuous Spirituality: Out from Fundamentalism.* New York: Crossroad, 1992.

———. *Speech, Silence, Action!: The Cycle of Faith.* Nashville: Abingdon, 1980.

———. *Women, Men, & the Bible.* Nashville: Abingdon, 1977.

———. *Women of Faith in Dialogue.* New York: Crossroad, 1987.

———. "The Women's Movement Challenges the Church." *The Journal of Psychology and Theology* 2, no. 4 (1974): 298–310.

Mollenkott, Virginia R., and Vanessa Sheridan. *Transgender Journeys.* Cleveland: Pilgrim, 2003.

Morgan, Marabel. *The Total Woman.* Old Tappan, NJ: F. H. Revell, 1973.

Neuer, Werner. *Man and Woman in Christian Perspective.* Wheaton, IL: Crossway, 1991.

Newsom, Carol A., and Sharon H. Ringe. *The Women's Bible Commentary.* Louisville: Westminster/John Knox, 1992.

O'Brien, William. "Handling Conflict: The Fallout from Fresno." *The Other Side* (December 1986): 25–41.

Olasky, Susan. "The Feminist Seduction of the Evangelical Church." *World* (1997): 12–15.

Osborne, Grant R. *The Hermeneutical Spiral: A Comprehensive Introduction to Biblical Interpretation.* Downers Grove, IL: InterVarsity, 1991.

Ostriker, Alicia. *Feminist Revision and the Bible.* The Bucknell Lectures in Literary Theory 7. Cambridge, MA: Blackwell, 1993.

Owings, Jeffrey. "Coming of Age in the 1990s" [on-line]. United States Department of Education (March 2002). Accessed 18 November 2005. Available from http://nces. ed.gov/pubs2002/200231pdf; Internet.

Packer, J. I. "Women, Authority and the Bible." In *Understanding the Differences*, ed. Alvera Mickelson. Downers Grove, IL: InterVarsity, 1986.

Patterson, Dorothy Kelley, and Rhonda Kelley, eds. *The Woman's Study Bible: The New King James Version.* Nashville: Thomas Nelson, 1995.

Phipps, William E. *Recovering Biblical Sensuousness.* Philadelphia: Westminster, 1975.

Pierce, Ronald R., and Rebecca Groothius, eds. *Discovering Biblical Equality*. Downers Grove, IL: Intervarsity, 2004.

Piper, John, and Wayne A. Grudem. *Recovering Biblical Manhood and Womanhood: A Response to Evangelical Feminism*. Wheaton, IL: Crossway, 1991.

Pride, Mary. *The Way Home: Beyond Feminism, Back to Reality*. Westchester, IL: Crossway, 1985.

Quebedeaux, Richard. *The Worldly Evangelicals*. San Francisco: Harper & Row, 1978.

Ramm, Bernard L. *Hermeneutics*. Grand Rapids: Baker, 1971.

Rich, Adrienne Cecile. *Compulsory Heterosexuality and Lesbian Existence*. London: Onlywomen Press, 1981.

———. *Of Women Born*. New York: Bantam, 1976.

Rothblatt, Martine Aliana. *The Apartheid of Sex: A Manifesto on the Freedom of Gender*. New York: Crown, 1995.

Ruether, Rosemary Radford. "Christian Tradition and Feminist Hermeneutics." In *The Image of God: Gender Models in Judaeo-Christian Tradition*, ed. Kari Elisabeth Børresen. Minneapolis: Fortress, 1995.

———. *Liberation Theology: Human Hope Confronts Christian History and American Power*. New York: Paulist, 1972.

———. *Sexism and God-Talk: Toward a Feminist Theology*. Boston: Beacon, 1983.

Russell, Letty M. *Feminist Interpretation of the Bible*. Philadelphia: Westminster, 1985.

———. *Human Liberation in a Feminist Perspective—a Theology*. Philadelphia: Westminster, 1974.

Saucy, Robert L., and Judith K. TenElshof. *Women and Men in Ministry: A Complementary Perspective*. Chicago: Moody, 2001.

Scanzoni, Letha. *Sexuality*. Philadelphia: Westminster, 1984.

Scanzoni, Letha, and Nancy Hardesty. *All We're Meant to Be: Biblical Feminism for Today*. Rev. ed. Nashville: Abingdon, 1986.

Scanzoni, Letha, and Virginia R. Mollenkott. *Is the Homosexual My Neighbor?: Another Christian View*. San Francisco: Harper & Row, 1978.

———. *Is the Homosexual My Neighbor?: Another Christian View*. Rev. ed. San Francisco: Harper & Row, 1994.

Scanzoni, Letha, and John H. Scanzoni. *Men, Women, and Change: A Sociology of Marriage and Family*. New York: McGraw-Hill, 1976.

Schungel-Straumann, Helen. "On the Creation of Man and Woman in Genesis 1–3: The History and Reception of the Texts Reconsidered." In *A Feminist Companion to the Bible*, ed. Athalya Brenner. Sheffield, England: Sheffield, 1993.

Schüssler Fiorenza, Elisabeth. *In Memory of Her: A Feminist Theological Reconstruction of Christian Origins*. New York: Crossroad, 1983.

Schüssler Fiorenza, Elisabeth, Shelly Matthews, and Ann Graham Brock. *Searching the Scriptures*. 2 vols. New York: Crossroad, 1993.

Scroggs, Robin. *The New Testament and Homosexuality: Contextual Background for Contemporary Debate*. Philadelphia: Fortress, 1983.

Siker, Jeffrey S. *Homosexuality in the Church: Both Sides of the Debate*. Louisville: Westminster/John Knox, 1994.

Smedes, Lewis B. *Sex for Christians: The Limits and Liberties of Sexual Living*. Grand Rapids: Eerdmans, 1976.

Spencer, Aída Besançon. *Beyond the Curse: Women Called to Ministry*. Nashville: Thomas Nelson, 1985.

Stanton, Elizabeth Cady. *The Woman's Bible*. Seattle: Coalition Task Force on Women and Religion, 1974.

———. *The Woman's Bible*. Boston: Northeastern University Press, 1993.

Stendahl, Krister. *The Bible and the Role of Woman*. Philadelphia: Fortress, 1966.

Strauch, Alexander. *Men and Women, Equal yet Different: A Brief Study of the Biblical Passages on Gender*. Littleton, CO: Lewis and Roth, 1999.

Study Bible for Women. Edited by Catherine Kroeger, Mary Evans, and Elaine Storkey. Grand Rapids: Baker, 1995.

Swidler, Leonard J. *Biblical Affirmations of Woman*. Philadelphia: Westminster, 1979.

Terrien, Samuel L. *Till the Heart Sings: A Biblical Theology of Manhood & Womanhood*. Philadelphia: Fortress, 1985.

Tong, Rosemarie. *Feminist Thought: A Comprehensive Introduction*. Boulder, CO: Westview, 1989.

Trager, James. *The Women's Chronology: A Year-by-Year Record from Prehistory to the Present*. New York: H. Holt, 1994.

Trible, Phyllis. *God and the Rhetoric of Sexuality: Overtures to Biblical Theology*. Philadelphia: Fortress, 1978.

Veith, Gene Edward. "Beyond Stealth." *World*, 29 January 2005, 30–31.

"Virginia Ramey Mollenkott" [on-line]. Accessed 14 March 2005. Available from http://www.geocities.com/vrmollenkott/?200514; Internet.

Williams, Delores S. *Sisters in the Wilderness: The Challenge of Womanist God-Talk*. Maryknoll, NY: Orbis, 1993.

Williams, Don. *The Bond That Breaks: Will Homosexuality Split the Church?* Los Angeles: BIM, 1978.

———. "Shall We Revise the Homosexual Ethic?" *Eternity*, May 1978, 46–48.

Winner, Lauren F. *Real Sex: The Naked Truth About Chastity*. Grand Rapids: Brazos, 2005.

Breinigsville, PA USA
20 July 2010
242084BV00001B/1/P